Assessing the Effectiveness of EAP Programmes

Editors: Andy Gillett and Liz Wray

BALEAP, London

www.baleap.org.uk

Assessing the Effectiveness of EAP Programmes

Edited by Andy Gillett and Liz Wray

First Published 2006

Published by: British Association of Lecturers in English for Academic Purposes, London, UK

Printed in the United Kingdom by Watford Printers

ISBN 978-0-9554874-0-8

Contents

EAP and success

Andy Gillett and Liz Wray, University of Hertfordshire

1. Introduction

The aim of EAP - English for Academic Purposes - is to help international students overcome some of the linguistic and cultural difficulties involved in studying through the medium of English. The objective of an EAP course, then, is for the students to learn the language and related skills to enable them to do this.

EAP is a branch of ESP in that the teaching content is explicitly matched to the language and study needs of the learners. It is also considered to be ESP if we take Robinson's (1991, pp. 2-5) features which are usually thought of as being typical defining characteristics of ESP courses.

- First, ESP is goal directed - the students are not learning the English language for the sake of it, but because they need to use English in their professional or academic lives. EAP students are usually current higher education students or they are hoping to go on to higher education after their EAP course. They need to learn English in order to succeed in their academic careers.

- Second, ESP courses are based on an analysis of needs, which aims to specify as closely as possible exactly what it is that the students have to do through the medium of English. One important feature of EAP courses is the close attention that is paid to students' aims and what they are studying or plan to study. The first stage in any EAP, and ESP, course, therefore, is to find out exactly why the students are learning English and what language and language skills they will need.

- Often there is a very clearly specified period for the ESP course. Most EAP students are doing fixed term courses in preparation for an academic course or they are studying English for a short time every week along with their academic courses.

- ESP learners tend to be adults rather than children. Most EAP students are over 18 and they will have made a difficult decision to study in an English medium university.

1

- Students may need specialist language, but this is not necessarily so. It is the linguistic tasks that the students will need to engage in that define the course. As with all ESP, an EAP lecturer would not take a text and ask, "What can I do with this text?" The starting point is always, "Why will my students need to read this text? What will my students need to do with this text and how can I help them to do it?"

- In some cases, a very high level of proficiency is not necessarily required, as long as the students can succeed in their aims. Students need to be able to understand their lectures, fellow students and textbooks and obtain good marks for assignments and examinations. The role of the EAP lecturer is to find ways to enable them to do this - getting their present tenses correct may not be as important as understanding the overall structure of the report they have to write.

The role of the EAP lecturer or course designer, then, is to find out what the students need, what they have to do in their academic courses, and help them to do this better in the time available. An adaptation of Bell (1981, p. 50) provides a useful model to do this (Figure 1).

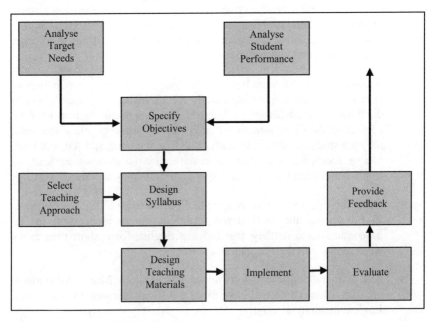

Figure 1: Course design model

2. Target Needs Analysis

The starting point is to analyse the students' target needs. This includes the language and related skills that they will need when they embark on their academic courses. They need to be clearly researched as different subjects at different levels in different institutions may have different needs (Hyland, 2000). However, some general statements can be made. The recent QAA benchmarking statement for languages (Quality Assurance Agency for Higher Education, 2002) identifies four key elements that characterise language programme outcomes: use of the target language; explicit knowledge of the language; knowledge of aspects of the target cultures and intercultural awareness. This is a useful framework in which to examine typical target needs.

2.1. Use of the target language

Typically, a student needs to use language in the following situations: lectures, seminars, tutorials, group projects, practical sessions, private study and examinations. In these situations, the language skills needed would include reading, writing, speaking and listening. Examples of the kinds of tasks that students would carry out are as follows. In lectures, they would, among other things, need to listen for general understanding, listen for specific points to remember, ask for clarification, read handouts and take notes. In seminars, they would listen and take notes, ask for more information, agree and disagree, and discuss, for instance. In practical sessions, it is necessary to listen to instructions, ask for information and clarification, read handouts and follow instructions, and write notes and reports (see Gillett, 1989, for more details).

The most problematic use of English in higher education is probably writing. Writing tasks vary from writing short answers in examinations to writing dissertations and theses. EAP courses often concentrate on the process of writing - planning, organising, presenting, re-writing, and proof-reading. Typical writing skills include research and using sources, writing different text types as well as different genres, and using an appropriate style. Students also need to do a large amount of reading, listening and note-taking. This must be done flexibly and involves surveying the text, skimming for gist or general impression, scanning to locate specifically required information as well as intensive study of specific sections of the text. Listening involves following a lecture or discussion, which means recognising lecture organisation and extracting relevant points to summarise. In both reading and listening, language skills such as understanding important points, distinguishing the main ideas from supporting detail, recognising unsupported claims and claims supported by evidence and following an argument are essential as are recognising known words and deducing the meaning of unfamiliar words and word groups from the context. Speaking is becoming increasingly important as teaching methods change to involve more group work. Making presentations involves producing and using notes, planning and presenting. Discussion includes interrupting politely, asking questions, agreeing and disagreeing. More recently, in addition, use of on-line discussion facilities of VLEs (Virtual Learning Environments) is becoming important (Gillett & Weetman, 2005).

2.2. Knowledge of language

More importantly, as well as teaching these skills, knowledge of the language that is used in these skills in the students' specific subject areas is necessary and forms an essential component of EAP courses. Recent research has provided us with useful data on academic language, both grammatical (Biber, Johansson, Leech, Conrad & Finegan, 1999) and lexical (Coxhead, 1998). This includes knowledge of different text types (oral and written) and features of different genres, linking words, signposting expressions, and appropriate style. Students also need knowledge of various strategies that they can use in comprehending written and oral texts and producing essays and oral presentations. As examinations and other forms of assessment are so important, knowledge of the format and language of exam questions is also necessary.

2.3. Culture and intercultural awareness

The culture where the language is used in EAP is higher education, usually, but not necessarily, in an English speaking country. Therefore, knowledge of the academic culture is necessarily part of an EAP course and students need to be aware of differences between their own academic cultures and the culture where they are studying. Writing conventions, such as organisation and use of sources, for example, can vary from country to country. While in the UK, students need to develop a willingness to accept responsibility for their own learning and to be reflective and critical. Other areas of difficulty include use of names between lecturers and students, how and when to ask questions and how to deal with lateness and privacy. As well as knowledge of the higher education culture in the UK, there are subject specific cultures (Hyland, 2000) that students and lecturers need to be aware of.

This information can be obtained in many ways: for example, looking at course documentation, looking at typical academic texts in the students' fields, talking to course leaders, talking to subject lecturers, talking to students, looking at students' work and looking at test and examination results. This is all part of the necessary preparation for any English for Academic Purposes course.

2.4. EAP/Study skills

There is often discussion whether these two terms - EAP and study skills - mean the same. We find it useful to make a distinction between general study skills that are not concerned with language and language study skills that will probably form part of an EAP course. There are many study skills books available and they usually concentrate on matters such as where to study, when to study, time management, remembering, developing study habits, filing and organising books, how to spend leisure time and so on, although they do often deal with aspects of study skills that involve language such as planning essays and taking notes. These general study skills are obviously important to our students in higher education, but they are not usually the main objective of EAP courses. The main objective of EAP courses is to teach the language, both general academic language and subject specific language as well as language related skills such as summarising and writing introductions. The language of the students' academic subject and language related study skills will form the main component of the EAP skills classes.

3. Student performance

After EAP lecturers and course designers have some knowledge of what the student will eventually need, they need to look at where the student is now, they have to analyse the students' present performance and knowledge. There are various ways in which this can be done. Most well-known are the commercial tests such as IELTS and TOEFL. Although, not EAP tests in the narrow sense, they are very widely used and provide some useful information.

The International English Language Testing System (IELTS) is jointly managed by the British Council, the University of Cambridge Local Examinations Syndicate and the International Development Program of Australian Universities and Colleges. It provides a systematic and continuously available system of assessing the English-language proficiency of non-native speakers who intend to study in the medium of English. The IELTS test is divided into four sub-tests: reading, writing, listening and speaking. A test report form gives details of the results of the test. Each sub-test is reported separately in the form of a band score. The individual sub-test band scores are added together and averaged to obtain an overall band score. Each band corresponds to a descriptive statement, which gives a summary of the English of a candidate classified at this level. The scale of bands increases from 1 to 9. This qualification is accepted by most British universities, who ask for levels of between 5.5 and 7 depending on subject and level of study. An intensive EAP course of around three months would normally be necessary to improve the students' IELTS scores by one band.

The Test of English as a Foreign Language (TOEFL) is a single subject examination recognised in most countries of the world as an indication of English proficiency for placement of students in colleges and universities. At the moment, there are three versions of the test, depending on which part of the world the test is taken in:

1. The traditional Paper-Based TOEFL test (PBT)

2. The Computer-Based TOEFL test. (CBT)

3. The Internet-Based TOEFL test (iBT)

Students are usually asked for at least 580 on the PBT, 233 on the CBT, or 90 on the iBT. These requirements are often increased to 600/250/100 or above for linguistically more demanding courses such as linguistics, literature or law.

As well as the commercial tests, there are many other kinds of tests available, many produced by university departments for their own use. Information about student performance can also be obtained, though, by talking to subject lecturers, examining student work, reading examiners reports or looking at exam marks, for example.

Furthermore, it is often felt that it is necessary to re-test the students once they arrive in the UK to obtain more detailed information about the students that broad-based test such as IELTS and TOEFL cannot provide.

4. Select teaching approach

Selecting the teaching approach requires knowledge of educational policies and practices and how people learn. There is a large amount of research available in this area, the largest amount being in the area of writing, especially the distinction between the product and process approaches to teaching writing (see Badger & White, 2000, Robinson, 1988). Most EAP teaching is task based, using the types of academic task commonly found in higher education and writing classes are usually based on some kind of extended writing task that the students do, with the help of in-class teaching and individual tutorial support. Listening to lectures, and other students in seminar situations, is difficult for students. It is especially difficult for students to listen and take relevant notes. A typical approach to teaching listening for academic purposes would involve doing large amounts of in-class listening, probably pre-recorded, helping the students to be more aware of typical language used in lectures as well as strategies for dealing with difficulties (see, for example, Flowerdew, 1994). Reading is similar with students doing large amounts of in-class and out of class reading, as well as the lecturer helping the students to be more aware of typical language used in academic texts, text structure and strategies for reading critically and dealing with difficulties (Clark, 1993; Cobb & Horst, 2001). Teaching speaking has received the least amount of published research (but see Weissberg, 1993), but a typical approach to teaching spoken English for academic purposes would again be tasked based with students taking part in seminar discussions and giving presentations, both supported by class teaching and individual tutorials.

5. Implementation

EAP courses are very often Pre-Sessional courses. That is, they are taken before the students' main academic courses start. Most universities in the UK offer these Pre-Sessional courses, which vary in length from one year to two weeks. The EAP courses frequently take place at the institution where the students intend to take their main academic course but this need not be the case. These courses are intended to prepare students coming to study in higher education in the UK to study in English. They also allow students to familiarise themselves with the new environment and facilities of the institution before their main courses start. The students need to learn to adopt particular approaches to their study and learn strategies and skills that will enable them to succeed in the British higher education system. The purpose of the Pre-Sessional EAP course is to bring the students up to the level that is necessary to start a course. In this case, EAP lecturers and course organisers need to liaise with admissions tutors to find out what is necessary. Some longer Pre-Sessional courses of up to, perhaps, one academic year – usually called foundation courses - attempt to prepare lower level students for entry to higher education. Some of these courses also include a quantity of academic subject content.

EAP courses can also be In-Sessional courses. That is they are taken at the same time as the students' main academic course. In-Sessional courses can take one of two forms. They can be either integrated into the students' academic study or be more general. The general classes can be seen as language support classes - these are usually free drop-in classes held at lunch-times or Wednesday afternoons and students attend when they are able. More recently, though, EAP courses are becoming embedded in the students' academic courses with EAP lecturers actually attending the students' lectures and seminars, and looking at current assignments, in order to offer relevant language support. Increasingly it

7

is also becoming possible for international students to take credit-bearing EAP courses as part of their degree.

6. Evaluation

There is already much information and research published on target needs analysis. There is also a large amount of research available on testing and evaluation of students and of particular teaching methods. Much of this research is in EAP. In a survey of EAP, Hamp-Lyons (2001) mentions needs analysis, analysis of linguistic and discoursal structures of academic texts for creating materials, effectiveness of teaching approaches, and assessment in EAP. But there is no mention of success; to what extent do our EAP programmes help our students succeed in their chosen academic fields.

The BALEAP (British Association of Lecturers in English for Academic Purposes) Professional Issues Meeting (PIM) held at the University of Hertfordshire on 24th June 2006 attempted to start to try to fill that gap by looking at research that has attempted to provide evidence that EAP course are helpful and what can be done to improve it and encourage it. As well as this, methods and techniques to do this research were also looked at.

Discussing research methods for evaluating language programmes, Lynch (1996) distinguishes between positivistic, or quantitative, design and naturalistic, or qualitative, design. According to Lynch, positivistic design is appropriate for measuring the effect of different methods on the success of the language programme. With a naturalistic design, the most common methods for gathering and recording data are "observation, interviews, journals, questionnaires, and document analysis. The data that are recorded by these methods can come from a variety of sources: students, instructors, administrators, evaluators, and other persons who interact with the program" (p. 107).

The papers at the PIM used most of these methods, with data from a wide range of sources to assess the success of EAP programmes.

7. Summary of papers

The first four contributors to this volume use naturalistic, or qualitative, design in order to gather data for their research. For all of them, the Pre-Sessional English course was central to their assessment of the effectiveness of EAP.

In the first phase of a project commenced in 2005, Barbara Atherton addresses the theme of academic success of the Pre-Sessional course at Kingston

University. In order to establish how successful the course is, she examines students' entry and exit test scores and post-course questionnaires. She reviews comments both from students who did and did not undertake Pre-Sessional English as they pursue follow-on degree programmes and also considers feedback from course directors. The data gathered suggests that the Pre-Sessional course at Kingston can be deemed successful and Atherton looks ahead to the next phase of the project which will address the issue of the provision of additional support for international students.

Diana Ridley reports on research designed to track students' progress and achievement following the Pre-Sessional course at the Sheffield Hallam University. She considers the relationship between students' exit scores and the length of time taken to complete academic programmes and also looks at ways of strengthening support for international students. She gathers data for her research from questionnaires, interviews, discussion and observation from both a student and lecturer perspective. Her findings suggest that the Pre-Sessional exit test does have predictive validity.

Mary Martala's case study questions the effectiveness of the writing component of the Pre-Sessional course at the University of Hertfordshire in preparing Chinese students for postgraduate study. Using data gathered from students' writing and responses to feedback questionnaires she concludes that the writing strand of the course does seem to equip students well for their further studies. A connection is made between assessment grades and learner attitude with the suggestion that a positive attitude to study plays a major part in educational success.

Chinese postgraduate students at Heriot-Watt University are the subject of the first stage of Nick Pilcher's research. Comments regarding the perceived effectiveness of EAP were gathered by interviewing a group of 21 students whilst undertaking dissertations in 2005. Although participants were generally positive about EAP provision, there is recognition that the complexity of the situation requires further data collection. It is acknowledged that tutors and departments need to work more closely together not only to gather additional data but also to develop the effectiveness of EAP.

The next two contributors take a positivistic, or quantitative, approach in assessing the effectiveness of EAP. The unreliability of band descriptors and the variability of a speaker's production prompt John Morley of the University of Manchester to examine alternative means for measuring oral proficiency gains over short Pre-Sessional courses. He considers the variables of fluency, accuracy and complexity and suggests that it may be possible to use certain of the measures he describes in order to gauge changes in oral proficiency over short periods.

Simon Kinzley of the University of Lancaster suggests that innovation theory may be combined with the appropriate collection and interpretation of data in assessing whether students are able to adopt the academic writing practices learned on Pre-Sessional courses as they proceed onto their degree programmes and whether adoption of these practices is linked to academic success. He claims that the methods he describes may be useful not only for other researchers, but also in establishing evidence surrounding the teaching of EAP.

Finally, Sonya Saunders presents a personal view of whether EAP works. She looks at many of the problems touched on in earlier papers and suggests ways forward for the future.

8. Conclusion

The PIM in June, with the title "Does EAP work?", therefore, provided a start to try to answer the question by looking at research that provided feedback that EAP succeeds. There is some evidence that it does, but there are still many methodological problems before we can really answer the question. We hope this will be a start and the publication of these papers will encourage more people to do the same.

References

Badger, R. & White, G. (2000). A process genre approach to teaching writing. *ELT Journal, 54,* 153-160.

Bell, R. (1981*). An introduction to applied linguistics: Approaches and methods in language teaching.* London: Batsford.

Biber, D., Johansson, S., Leech, G., Conrad, S. & Finegan, E. (1999). *Longman grammar of spoken and written English.* Harlow: Longman.

Clark, R. J. (1993). Developing practices of resistance: Critical reading for students of politics. In D. Graddol, L. Thompson, & M. Byram (Eds.), *Language and culture* (pp. 113-122). Clevedon, Avon: BAAL and Multilingual Matters.

Cobb, T. & Horst, M. (2001). Reading academic English: Carrying learners across the lexical threshold. In J. Flowerdew & M. Peacock (Eds.), *Research perspectives on English for academic purposes* (pp. 315-329). Cambridge: Cambridge University Press.

Coxhead, A. (1998). *An academic word list.* Wellington: Victoria University of Wellington.

Flowerdew, J. (Ed.). (1994). *Academic listening: Research perspectives.* Cambridge: Cambridge University Press.

Gillett, A. J. (1989). Designing an EAP course: English language support for further and higher education. *Journal of Further and Higher Education, 13*(2), 92-104.

Gillett, A. J. & Weetman, C. (2005). Investigation of the perceived usefulness of a StudyNet group discussion facility by students in higher education. *Journal for the Enhancement of Learning and Teaching, 2,* 36-43.

Hamp-Lyons, L. (2001). English for academic purposes. In R. Carter & D. Nunan (Eds.), *The Cambridge guide to teaching English to speakers of other languages* (pp. 126-130). Cambridge: Cambridge University Press.

Hyland, K. (2000). *Disciplinary discourses.* Harlow: Longman.

Lynch, B. K. (1996). *Language program evaluation.* Cambridge: Cambridge University Press.

Quality Assurance Agency for Higher Education (2002). *Subject benchmark statements: Languages and related studies.* Available from; http://www.qaa.ac.uk/academicinfrastructure/benchmark/honours/

Robinson, P. (1991). *ESP today: A practitioner's guide.* London: Prentice Hall.

Robinson, P. C. (Ed.). (1988). *Academic writing: Process and product (*ELT Documents 129*).* London: Modern English Publications.

Weissberg, B. (1993). The graduate seminar: Another research process genre. *English for Specific Purposes, 12,* 23-36.

Balancing needs: How successful can a Pre-Sessional course be?

Barbara Atherton, Kingston University

Abstract

In seeking to establish the success of any course, the criteria used must acknowledge the differing needs and expectations of the various stakeholders and recognise that there is more to the concept of success than passing or failure. This paper focuses on the impact of the pre-sessional 'valued added' elements which can be said to underpin academic success, drawing from data from the first year of a small-scale research project designed to assess the effectiveness of Kingston's Pre-Sessional English language course.

The entry and exit scores of the 125 students attending Pre-Sessional 2005 are reviewed and the level of satisfaction expressed in the end-of-course questionnaire is compared to the students' comments as they progressed through their academic courses. These comments are contrasted with those of students who did not attend a Pre-Sessional course and with responses from Course Directors. Although conclusions at this stage can only be tentative, overall course pass rates and levels of satisfaction appear good. The importance of strategies to aid students' integration into the academic and social community is noted, as is the differing attitudes to the advancement of students' academic English language skills.

In the light of the findings so far, the paper concludes with recommendations for Pre-Sessional 2006 and for further research into ways of continuing to support our students and colleagues.

1. Introduction

In 2005, Kingston University's Pre-Sessional course became part of the offer condition for all international students not meeting the University's English language entry requirements. Progression was to be seamless, so the offer was for applicants to attend rather than pass the course and all applicants, irrespective of their age, nationality and previous academic backgrounds, were required to attend a 4-week Pre-Sessional block for each 0.5 IELTS shortfall. Given that this element of the admissions policy was now to rely totally on IELTS/TOEFL results, with the underlying implication that all students would take the same time to develop the required language and academic skills to meet their offer conditions, it was important to design a project which set out to address the question: *How successful can a Pre-Sessional be?*

But how should success be defined? A student who has passed a course is deemed to be successful - simple, to the point and apparently obvious but, as

12

Rea-Dickins & Germaine (1992, p. 6-7) remind us, any evaluation must consider not only *what* our students achieve but the *why* and *how* which underpin this achievement. What level of pass was achieved, with what additional help and support and from whom? How did students view their experience, (particularly important in these days of student satisfaction surveys and league tables); did the results reflect the students' true abilities? We also have a responsibility to two other significant 'client groups' - the University who looks to the Pre-Sessional to support international student recruitment and our academic colleagues in the students' receiving Schools who expect Pre-Sessional students to be well prepared for their future academic programmes. In attempting to measure success then, it is necessary to consider the needs and expectations of all our stakeholders and the factors that impact on their perceptions of success.

The project set out to address these questions with data collected from questionnaires and structured interviews with Pre-Sessional students, other international students attending our In-Sessional English Language Support Programme, who had not attended the Pre-Sessional and interviews with Course Directors[1]. This paper presents the initial findings from the first year's results and hence is still very much work in progress. Following a brief introduction to the course and students on Pre-Sessional 2005, their entry and exit scores, views on the course and comments from them and other students as they progressed through their first year with us are reviewed to establish how successful the course was from the students' perspective. The views of a sample number of Course Directors are summarised and the paper concludes with a short rationale for the key changes implemented for Pre-Sessional 2006 and for the next stage of the research.

2. Kingston's Pre-Sessional

The course is designed on a weekly project task based syllabus. Each week starts with a project briefing and ends with students giving a presentation, taking part in a seminar and writing an essay or report. Students are divided into postgraduate and undergraduate groups and, as far as possible, by faculty, thus facilitating development of academic subject specific vocabulary, discourse types and other academic-related requirements. Language and study skills are mapped onto each weekly theme to form an indicative syllabus and the emphasis is on applied language development within, as far as is possible, the context of the students' academic subject disciplines.

Students receive marks and formative feedback on their weekly presentations, seminar skills and written work. The end of course result is based on a review of the marks gained in the preceding weeks, against a list of 'can do' statements on the end of course report and particularly, on the students' performance in the last 2 weeks of the course. There is no final examination. Students are given a percentage mark, using the University's percentage grade descriptors. It is important to note that these scores are not reflecting an IELTS correlation, but are the course team's judgement as to how well prepared these students are for their future academic courses.

14 students attended our 12-week course, 44 enrolled for the 8-week and 67 for the 4-week, giving an overall total of 125, all but 2 of whom were progressing on to undergraduate or postgraduate degrees at Kingston. Altogether, 25 different nationalities were represented. The largest national group (21) came from Korea, mostly going on to courses in Art & Design, 18 came from Japan, again mainly to study Art & Design. The majority of the 17 students from Thailand were to study postgraduate courses at Kingston Business School and the 16 post and undergraduate students from China were progressing to courses in Business, Economics or the Arts & Social Sciences.

Although most arrived having taken an IELTS or TOEFL test they were given a short entry test on the first day and this mark was compared to the students' 'official' language qualification. The same test is also used for our In-Sessional courses so over the years it has been possible to develop an unofficial correlation with IELTS and TOEFL scores. Significant discrepancies between the official test scores and our own were noted across nationality groups, especially with scores obtained from tests taken in China and Korea; two of our three Russians did particularly badly on the KU test.

Analysis of the two sets of test scores (presented in Table 1 below) identified those students on the officially 'correct course', those who should have been on longer/shorter courses according to their official test score and those for whom we had 'cause for concern'. These were students we felt potentially faced a significant challenge – either because their official test score showed they were on too short a course or as a result of our own initial assessment.

	Correct course	Longer/shorter	Cause for concern	
12 week (14 sts)	12	2 longer	3	21%
8 week (44 sts)	28	8 longer 8 shorter	15	34%
4 week (68 sts)	54	9 longer 5 no need	23	33%

Table 1: Analysis of entry test scores

The final 4 weeks of the Pre-Sessional therefore started with 125 students, 41 of whom were on a course which ideally was too short to enable them and us to meet the course objectives successfully.

Despite these reservations, the end of course results showed that perhaps we were unduly pessimistic in our first assessment. 117 students passed, 4 postgraduates and 1 undergraduate failed and 4 students dropped out to return home for personal or family matters, unrelated to Kingston or the Pre-Sessional. Some students made quite considerable progress in all aspects of the course. The majority worked very hard, formed supportive peer groups and took advantage of the significant amount of individual and small group tutorial help provided throughout the course. However, only 2 undergraduates achieved 70% and no postgraduate students achieved 70%; 12 undergraduates and 28 postgraduates achieved marks of 60% or over, and over half the cohort were awarded grades which are effectively saying that, whilst having passed the course, they are still likely to require considerable support as they embark on their academic programmes.

3. The 'causes for concern'

The number of students identified at the start of the course as 'causes for concern' reduced to 28, but this is still high at 22% of the cohort and is significant when considering the extent to which the course can be said to be meeting the needs of both the students and their receiving Schools. Although they have now achieved the course objectives, their level of success is judged to be 'fragile'. They may have made good, and in many cases, excellent progress but questions remain as to how long lasting this improvement will be and whether they can and will adopt the study strategies we have taught them. There may be questions about their ability to function at the speed and/or level of accuracy and academic rigour required by their academic courses and hence whether they will be able to achieve their academic potential. Our experience has shown that rapid progress made on a highly intensive and supportive Pre-Sessional usually requires a sustained period of subsequent practice and reinforcement, a factor that is so often outside the control of the Pre-Sessional course team.

However, the course can be said to have been successful in terms of overall pass/fail rates and hence from the University's point of view, in terms of the number of international students who progressed on to their academic courses. To establish the students' views, the results of the end-of-course questionnaire were analysed and followed up by a further questionnaire and interviews.

4. The Pre-Sessional experience – the students' views

The end of course questionnaire asks students to rate how well they felt they had achieved the overarching course objectives. A rating of 1 equals not achieved and 6 equals fully achieved. Note that only 71 responses were received from the 125 participants:

Pre-Sessional Objectives	1 = Not achieved %	2	3	4	5	6 = Fully achieved %
1. To develop the students' academic English language skills	1		7	37	39.5	15.5
2. To give students experience in the methods and study skills used in British universities			10	27	39	24
3. To develop students' confidence in their own use of the English language			10	32.5	46.5	14
4. To introduce students to aspects of Britain and the British way of life		9	8	32	38	13

Table 2: Achievement of course objectives

Although the responses to Objective 4 were disappointing (as was attendance at the range of activities aimed to facilitate these aspects), it seems reasonable to suggest that the students thought that the course was working well. The results together with the additional comments on the questionnaires certainly supported the overwhelming reaction of the students as they left us for the start of the academic year, so at this stage, Pre-Sessional 2005 can also be regarded as a 'success' for its participants. The majority felt that they had developed their academic English language skills, they had gained experience of studying in the UK and they had developed confidence.

4.1. Five months on

The acid test comes when we look at how these students integrated and performed once they joined their academic programmes; how they coped with their courses and life at Kingston.

Students were therefore sent a follow up questionnaire at the start of Semester 2, and although the response rate was very disappointing with only 24 replies out of a total cohort of 125, these students replied in some detail and, together with the interviews conducted with the research groups, a picture begins to emerge. Responses to the key questions are summarised in Table 3.

	1 = Strongly disagree /24	2	3	4	5	6 = Strongly agree /24
I think that the Pre-Sessional enabled me to start my course with confidence		1	3	8	6	6
I understood what my lecturers wanted me to do		1	3	7	8	5
I feel I can cope with my studies			9	6	5	2
I was well informed about life at Kingston		1	4	3	5	11
I know where to get help if necessary			5		13	6

Table 3: Follow up questionnaire

Satisfaction rates still appear reasonably good (although with the low response rate it could be argued that those who were dissatisfied declined to answer), and half way through the academic year the students' view is still generally one of a successful Pre-Sessional experience overall although real life is now cutting in. A number of students and their Course Directors were therefore asked to consider their successes and problems as they progressed through into the final stages of their first year at Kingston, providing key factors which can contribute to the concept of 'success'.

5. A sense of belonging: confidence and friendships

Our students continued to feel that the Pre-Sessional gave them confidence and prepared them well for what was to follow, a view which was supported by comments from their receiving Schools. They generally settled in more quickly than those who did not attend the course. However, several had their confidence dented. They commented on the problems encountered after moving from the highly-supportive Pre-Sessional environment, where everyone was an international student to one where native speakers were in the majority. Pre-Sessional students reported feeling excited but some, joining large course cohorts, reported feeling scared, shocked, and nervous during Induction Week and took between 1 - 3 months to 'feel at home'. They did, however, fare better than the Non Pre-Sessional students (NPSs) interviewed who, whilst also excited, said they felt confused, disorientated, lonely and lost.

The importance of friendships cannot be underestimated and the Pre-Sessional students readily acknowledged the value of the friends they had made on the course and the fact that they already knew people to ask for help if required. They also generally went on to make more friends within their course groups or with other international students than the NPSs. Making friends with native speakers, however, proved difficult for the majority of non-European international students. Forland & Kingston (2004, p.5) note the importance of cultural synergy and that isolation from native speakers can cause "feelings of depression ... and lead to students failing or dropping out of their courses". Significantly, the majority of the students interviewed so far for this project expressed a preference for remaining with Pre-Sessional friends or students from their own cultures and had little wish to extend their social network. They also expressed a reluctance to join sports and social clubs or to engage in the 'drinking culture' which tends to predominate amongst many first year home students staying in halls of residence. This 'barrier to integration' is noted in the UKCOSA Survey (2004, p. 69) but the authors also point out that home students tend to make and maintain friendships outside rather than inside the classroom (p.67). Despite, or perhaps because of this, both Pre-Sessional and NPSs groups commented on the difficulty of understanding the home students and some Pre-Sessional students said that they would have liked to mix more with native speakers and to use English socially during the Pre-Sessional.

6. Knowing what is expected

Hartill (2000, p. 128) identifies the importance of international students knowing what will be expected of them when they start their academic courses. Our Pre-Sessional students felt that they were clear about what their lecturers wanted them to do and generally felt that the course had prepared them well or extremely well for their assessments. They felt they had an advantage over other new students, as they knew the layout of the campuses, the Learning Resources Centres and ICT systems. Course Directors too feel that Pre-Sessional students are better prepared for their courses than the other international students, are generally more relaxed, confident and 'trusting of the institution'. As one Course Director commented: "They know that what they are being asked to do is for a reason; they know what is expected". This advantage is generally estimated to last for at least a month and 'possibly longer'.

However, it is worrying to see from the questionnaire (Table 3 above) that 14 students felt unsure or very unsure about whether they could cope with their studies, a response reinforced by the 'wish list' of what, in retrospect, students would have liked to spend more time on during their Pre-Sessional. This list included: more time spent on planning for essay/report writing - an interesting request as this is an area many seem to resist during the course; writing of essays and reports (borne out by the end of course questionnaire) and on presentations and seminars. Also flagged was more help with reading skills in general, reading around academic subjects and vocabulary development.

7. Accessing Support

All students spoke highly of the support given by lecturers and Course Directors and indeed our academic colleagues estimate that they spend between 25% - 65% more time with international students. This estimate increases significantly for those supervising postgraduate dissertations. Most students also used and praised the University's learning management system, Blackboard.

There is a marked difference, however, between Pre and Non Pre-Sessional students' attitudes to the continued development of their English and use of in-sessional support. Whilst we would have hoped that the Pre-Sessional students would wish to continue to develop their language skills (and indeed that we had furnished them with the skills to do this) it is apparent from many interviewed that English is now merely a facilitator – an adjunct to their academic studies. Strategies for the speedy and successful processing of their course work, and for mixing with their friends are important but there is little wish to develop their knowledge over and above that which is absolutely necessary for their work. They are looking back at handouts and materials from the Pre-Sessional course and seeking help on an individual basis from members of the academic English team, but very few are attending classes. Additionally, they have been found to be far more demanding of these classes and if these do not meet their immediate needs, the students tended not to return. By contrast, many NPS students see the further development of their general and academic language skills as a valuable addition to their academic studies and regularly attend the In-Sessional provision. Interestingly, the NPSs also tend to attribute any difficulties encountered to 'language problems' whereas the Pre-Sessional students now take a wider view, identifying both the academic and linguistic challenges. However, the non-attendance at In-Sessional classes is an obvious issue, particularly for those students who passed the Pre-Sessional with low scores and for those identified as 'causes for concern'. Perhaps inevitably, they were also the students who were difficult to contact during the research period, who did not reply to e-mails, and were rarely seen around the University. When seen, it was apparent that some had made very little progress with their language skills this year and may even have gone backwards.

This was particularly noticeable in academic disciplines where students spend a considerable amount of time working in self-selected groups on independent or small group projects. One Thai postgraduate student estimated that from using English all day on the Pre-Sessional, he now uses it for only 1 hour a day; he works in a Thai restaurant most evenings and mixes almost exclusively with Thai friends from the Pre-Sessional. A Korean undergraduate student now lives in the local Korean community and, whilst using English for 4 hours a day on the two days he is in the University, admits to either not using it or using it for reading only for an hour or two a day. These examples are not unusual. Several students admitted accessing sources on the internet in their own languages and then 'translating' when preparing their assignments, increasing their reliance on their first language and exposing them to the risk of 'forced' errors resulting from the translation process. For these and students in similar situations there is now little opportunity to consolidate and practise the new language which was acquired so intensively on the Pre-Sessional. When asked about their progress their list of problems reflected many of the 'cost' factors identified by Banerjee (2003) cited in Banerjee & Wall (2006, p. 56) with difficulties in understanding native speaker speech and processing materials for assignments again coming to the fore.

Other academic courses are able to require much more active use of the language on a regular basis and efforts are made to integrate students from different nationalities across study groups. Whilst this has been known to cause problems, especially at undergraduate level with international students frustrated by the casual attitude of native speaking students and native speakers frustrated by the poor level of English of some international students, they are required to use the language skills they acquired and hence do continue to make progress. Whilst this 'faculty effect' is difficult to counter, if is nevertheless, another factor which can impact on the longer term assessment of Pre-Sessional success, particularly in terms of the perception of the course across the University community as a whole.

8. Changes for Pre-Sessional 2006

Although this project was still in its early days, a review of the 2005 course led to several changes for Pre-Sessional 2006, the most significant of which was an increase in course lengths to 15, 10 and 5-week courses. The rationale for this change was centred on this year's results, views of academic colleagues and the recognition that students coming in with IELTS 5.0 or 5.5, especially progressing onto postgraduate courses, require a more sustained period of time for both learning and consolidation. There is also an increasing acknowledgement that, whilst some in our international student community may be 'good language learners' after Naiman, Fröhlich, Stern & Todesco (1978), the majority may no longer fall into this category and adequate time to prepare prior to the start of their academic programmes is more important than ever.

The ability to cope, to manage the pace and variety of tasks required, is a recurring theme when talking to international students, exemplified by their excuse that they would come to in-sessional support classes if they had more time. Forland & Kingston (2004) also note the Catch 22 problem of students saying they do not have time to access the very support designed to assist their studies and the Kingston students interviewed estimated that it takes them between 50% - 70% longer to do course and assessment work than their native speaking counterparts, mainly as a result of the time taken to undertake the reading required for each assignment. Anecdotal evidence does, however, suggest that many students who attended the shorter Pre-Sessional courses may be reluctant to adopt the advice given to them and are unable or unwilling to accept the need to change their approach and study patterns. This would seem to be a valuable area for further research.

In response to student feedback, adjustments have been made to the timetable to enable a more flexible use of time and integration of language and study skills, providing 4-hour blocks for academic writing/reading and research skills, hence reinforcing the planning, research, writing relationship. This should be additionally enhanced by the slight reduction in the assessment load, with students now having 2 weeks to complete some projects. It is also hoped to provide more native speaker involvement by increasing the number of guest lectures, as part of the social programme and including discussion groups with the students.

9. Conclusion

All members of BALEAP are very clear that Pre-Sessional courses are not IELTS preparation courses; neither are they 'grammar crammers'. Whilst we aim for all students to achieve the right level of academic English language ability, we also seek to provide them with a level of familiarity and competency with the 'academic system' which will, it is hoped, help them overcome any linguistic shortfall and hence enable them to successfully achieve their academic objectives. Any conclusions from the first year of this project can only be tentative but the majority of the participants felt they had had a successful experience and all but 4 of the students with lower than the required English language entry levels, did progress onto their academic courses at Kingston, thereby meeting our overarching objectives and those of the University. When asked to rate their own priorities, our Course Directors have, to date, placed equal emphasis on the development of the students' academic English language skills and the development of confidence. They are generally satisfied with the Pre-Sessional, but it is clear that they and their course teams are still required to provide a considerable amount of additional time and support to all their international students.

We do therefore appear to be balancing the needs of our stakeholders, we do have a successful Pre-Sessional and changes made now and in the future will ensure that the course continues and builds on this success. We know that the Pre-Sessional works at the level of getting the students onto their courses, but with what level of success, with what additional help and support and with what quality of experience are the questions for the next phase of the project.

Note:

[1]Further details of the project design and data collection methods can be obtained from the author by e-mailing B.Atherton@kingston.ac.uk

References

Banerjee, J. & Wall, D. (2006). Assessing and reporting performances on pre-sessional EAP courses: Developing a final assessment checklist and investigating its validity. *Journal of English for Academic Purposes, 5,* 50 -69.

Forland, H. & Kingston, E. (2004). Bridging the gap in expectations between international students and academic staff – "at home the teachers feed me with knowledge, but in the UK they help me pick up the spoon and learn to feed myself!" Paper presented at the European Education Research

Association's (EERA) European Conference on Educational Research (ECER), University of Crete, Rethymnon, Crete, September 2004.

Hartill, J. (2000). Assessing postgraduates in the real world. In G. M. Blue, J. Milton & J. Saville, (Eds.), *Assessing English for academic purposes* (pp. 117-130). Oxford: Peter Lang.

Naiman, N., Fröhlich, M., Stern H. H. & Todesco, A. (1978). *The Good language learner.* Toronto: OISE.

Rea-Dickens, P. & Germaine, K. (1992). *Evaluation.* Oxford: Oxford University Press.

UKCOSA (2004). *Broadening our horizons: International students in UK universities and colleges.* London: UKCOSA.

Is English language proficiency the barrier to success?

Tracking a cohort of Pre-Sessional students at Sheffield Hallam University

Diana Ridley, University of Sheffield

Abstract

In this paper I will report on a research project that took place at Sheffield Hallam University (SHU) between January 2000 and December 2002. Internal funding was made available for the research after concern had been expressed by some academic staff over the progress and achievement of a number of international students who speak English as an additional language. The project addressed two main research questions:

- Is there a relationship between Pre-Sessional exit test results and subsequent academic course completion?
- How can current support for international students be strengthened?

This paper focuses on how the first question was addressed by the research. A cohort of students who had completed the Pre-Sessional course at SHU in the summer of 2000 was tracked. Data was obtained from an examination of 1) Pre-Sessional exit test scores and 2) student performance on academic courses.

The study revealed that 84% of the Pre-Sessional students from the summer of 2000 did in fact complete their academic courses although there was a considerable delay for some. In the paper I will outline the relationship which became apparent between Pre-Sessional exit scores and the length of time taken for academic course completion. The findings also highlighted the significance of providing support for international students, both on EAP In-Sessional and Pre-Sessional programmes, and on academic courses.

1. Introduction

In this paper, I will report on a tracking project which took place at Sheffield Hallam University (SHU) between 2000 and 2002. I will first of all outline the concerns amongst academic staff which gave rise to the project and then present the study, including the research questions, the sample of students who were the focus of the research, the methods of data collection and the findings.

2. Is English language proficiency the barrier to success on academic courses?

Prior to the research project, concern had been expressed by a number of academic tutors about the English language proficiency of some international students on academic courses. The quotes below illustrate the nature of their disquiet.

> *(The students) who have got English as an entry requirement and if you like, just about meet it, they seem to struggle, particularly in that first semester.*

> *To say it (English language proficiency) is an issue, it's an issue when you can't understand what the student is saying. And it does come out in the exams. It's very hard again with the large number of students and you try to engage them all in debates, it's very hard to pick up on what their actual skill is, language wise, it's very difficult to do that, you get them to comment, often you ask them a question and you get a long pause and sometimes you just think well I've just got to move on. I'm aware that by picking on people in the class you can undermine their confidence and you can get into all sorts of trouble in that way so I've got a tendency if someone doesn't like answering questions, not to ask them questions which can be quite problematic on picking up on their language skills.*

> *They do struggle with this notion of what we understand by academic writing on our courses at postgraduate level and they do struggle ... at times with their lack of development of English language skills so when they practically come to write down their ideas it's not always the quality that one would expect, let's put it that way.*

As a result of these concerns, academic tutors expressed an interest in knowing the level of English language proficiency that should be required of international students in order to ensure success on their courses. Amongst English-medium universities around the world, there are many differences in the stipulated requirements for demonstrating English language proficiency and preparedness for study. Some may insist on a certain level of performance on an external test such as IELTS whereas others may offer students a place on a course if they satisfactorily complete a Pre-Sessional EAP course offered by the university (Banerjee & Wall, 2006).

Is English language proficiency the barrier to success?

After interviewing admissions tutors as part of the SHU research project, it was clear that there was an awareness that a student applying to study at the University should show competence in reading and developing arguments in writing, and not just speaking.

> *...they have to be able to interpret concepts and write about them, reproduce models, think conceptually in another language. What we don't know of course is what level of English, measure in terms of a test, what sort of level should they have of writing ability to be able to do that. Because they might appear adequate in terms of being able to speak English and understand it but we don't know what sort of competence you actually need to be able to write conceptually in another language.*

There appeared to be increased attention being paid by admissions tutors to the particular English language proficiency qualification that a student has, with IELTS becoming more popular because of its focus on the different language skills, speaking, listening, reading and writing.

> *The fact that they can speak fluently doesn't necessarily mean that they could read academic texts in English and then make use of that information. And that's where it's so difficult and short of setting them an assignment to do in class I can't think of quite what else we can do so IELTS, we do take TOEFL as well but more and more IELTS because as I understand it, it tests more in distinct areas than TOEFL does.*

> *We're emphasising a lot more now, not just conversation, understanding but we're particularly focusing on their writing skills in IELTS because sometimes the writing skills are low and the other parts are high. Therefore the overall score might be 6, it might be only a 5 on the writing skills, it might be a 7 elsewhere. So we're taking a more close look at the components that make up that IELTS score.*

One tutor questioned the morality of accepting students who are likely to struggle on an academic course for English language proficiency reasons. The difficulty is being able to determine whether, by requiring a higher level of English language proficiency, one would be excluding some students who could in fact succeed.

> *We've been wondering about whether we ask for high enough entry. ... clearly what people can understand and do is crucial to how they get on*

on the course. And it's soul destroying, if you think if you spend 8, 9, 10 grand on your course fees and your airfare and then you've got to live here for a year. Financially the investment is huge and the moral and personal investment in coming here and failing and it's hugely unethical of us not to ensure that we've done our best to make sure that they've at least a reasonable chance of passing.

Arising from these concerns some funding was made available from the University to explore the issues surrounding the English language proficiency of international students who are accepted to study on academic courses. There have already been a number of small scale studies done in UK universities in this vein which have investigated the relationship between English language proficiency on entry and performance on academic courses. For example, in some research at Lancaster University, Joan Allwright and Jay Banerjee (1997) compared IELTS scores on entry and results on academic courses. They talk about risk of failure. With a sample of 38 postgraduate students who had attended the Pre-Sessional course they concluded that an IELTS 7 was required for there to be no risk at all of failure. For scores below IELTS 7, the relationship between language proficiency and performance on academic courses was not straightforward. Seven out of ten students who were below the university requirement of IELTS 6, gained clear passes. Nevertheless, language proficiency was perceived by academic staff to be a difficulty for students who fell both slightly above and below IELTS 6 in the sense that it hindered their academic progress. From the statistics gathered and also questionnaire and interview data, Allwright and Banerjee concluded that there are many different factors which influence academic success and failure and these can not be isolated to language proficiency.

Alan Tonkyn (1995) cites a number of researchers who support this point, in particular, Sen (1970), who argued that factors such as learning background, preparedness for and adaptation to study and life in the UK, health, and the financial circumstances of students have a major influence on academic success and these are often more important than language proficiency. In the light of these arguments and the above quotes from academic staff, it would appear that EAP Pre-Sessional courses have a clear role to play, not only in raising English language proficiency but also in preparing international students for study in English medium universities by familiarising them with the expectations and conventions on academic courses.

Gill Meldrum (1996), with the aim of evaluating and confirming the validity of Pre-Sessional exit assessments, examined the relationship between exit bandings on the Pre-Sessional course at the University of Nottingham and performance on academic courses. She was looking at the predictive validity of the exit bandings, i.e. whether the bandings are effective predictors of academic success, and at the concurrent validity of the exit bandings by comparing the pass rates of students with the different Pre-Sessional exit bandings with the pass rates of students who had comparable TOEFL or IELTS scores. Although Meldrum acknowledged the contributions of other variables as well as English language proficiency to academic success, she found from her tracking of 257 students over two years that 88% of the Pre-Sessional students had passed and 84% of the students who had been accepted with other 'language' qualifications had passed. Meldrum therefore felt able to conclude that the Pre-Sessional exit bandings are effective predictors of success on an academic course and that they are broadly comparable to IELTS and TOEFL scores.

In the study at SHU, it became apparent that there was concern amongst the academic tutors connected with admissions that the exit test result from the Pre-Sessional course should accurately reflect whether a student can cope with an academic course. Concern was expressed as to whether the Pre-Sessional exit assessments equate with IELTS scores. Despite the fact that research has shown that the writing requirements on a course in HE are different from the writing skills demonstrated in an IELTS test (Moore & Morton, 2005), there is still a desire on the part of many admissions tutors to be able to benchmark a Pre-Sessional course result with an internationally recognised external test score. As the Pre-Sessional course at Sheffield Hallam University began in 1998, at the start of this research project in 2000, the Pre-Sessional assessments had not become fully established and accepted within the University. Consequently, a study such as that conducted by Meldrum seemed an effective way to provide evidence that the end of Pre-Sessional course assessment was a valid way to predict whether a student would be able to succeed on an academic course. As Banerjee & Wall (2006) point out, approaches to assessment on Pre-Sessional courses vary considerably amongst universities and therefore the validity and reliability of an assessment process has to be demonstrated and recognised within the individual institution in which it is used.

In its original format, the exit test on the Pre-Sessional course at SHU included a listening test, a speaking test, a written project and an oral presentation based on the project. Academic departments were advised to accept students who achieved 60% or above on the exit test. Data collected from tracking the summer 2000 Pre-Sessional students revealed the extent to which there was correlation between exit test results and performance on academic courses. These results were intended to serve two purposes: firstly, to suggest the Pre-

Sessional exit test levels we should be looking for in order to predict likely success and secondly, to show whether the Pre-Sessional exit test is a valid and reliable measure comparable to an IELTS band.

3. Research questions

The following two questions were formulated for the research project as a whole.

1. Is there a relationship between Pre-Sessional exit test results and subsequent academic course completion?
2. How can current support for international students be strengthened?

The second question was felt to be important to address the anxieties expressed by academic staff, given that previous research had indicated that it is difficult to establish a clear cut relationship between the English language proficiency entry scores and success on academic courses. In an article published in 2004, I explore many of the issues which emerged when addressing the second question (Ridley, 2004). The current paper, however, focuses on the first question.

It is important to point out that although it is widely acknowledged that a Pre-Sessional assessment or exit test assesses much more than language proficiency, it is still often perceived to be a measure of competence in English language, as are the results of international tests such as IELTS and TOEFL. In this paper, my intention is not to suggest that the Pre-Sessional exit test is solely a language proficiency measure although as the research was set up to address concerns about English language proficiency, on occasions, it may appear that this is what I am doing.

4. Data collection methods

The cohort of Pre-Sessional students who attended the Pre-Sessional course in the summer of 2000 was tracked whilst completing their academic courses at Sheffield Hallam University. Due to some difficulties in collecting consistent information about their progress on their courses, the decision was made to compare their Pre-Sessional exit test results with the time of their academic course completion.

In addition to this, to ascertain how current support could be strengthened, interviews were conducted with both students and academic staff, and questionnaires were circulated to Pre-Sessional students on four occasions throughout the academic year after their Pre-Sessional course. The intention was to gain greater insights into academic course expectations and the experiences of students on their academic courses. However, as mentioned, the focus of this paper is on the findings from the data collected to address the first research question.

5. Tracking the summer 2000 Pre-Sessional students

Forty eight students finished the Pre-Sessional course in the summer of 2000. Table 1 below illustrates the gender and nationality distribution of the course participants.

Nationality	Number of men	Number of women	Total
Taiwanese	9	15	24
Chinese	1	1	2
Thai	0	3	3
Indonesian	1	0	1
Japanese	0	4	4
Libyan	6	0	6
Omani	1	0	1
Saudi	3	0	3
United Arab Emirates	1	0	1
Yemeni	1	0	1
Venezuelan	0	1	1
German	1	0	1

Table 1: Nationality and gender distribution of students attending the summer 2000 Pre-Sessional course

Thirty eight of these students went on to do Master's courses at Sheffield Hallam University. Two of the remaining ten students completed one semester exchange programmes, and eight did not continue at SHU. Five of these eight students had low exit scores (below 60%) on the final test, one did not take the test and two achieved over 60% on the exit test but had alternative plans.

Table 2 shows the academic course destinations of the thirty eight students who continued at SHU.

Course title	Number of students
MSc International Marketing	8
MSc International Business Management	5
MBA	2
MSc Human Resource Management	1
MA Banking and Finance	5
MBA Industrial Management	5
MSc Advanced Engineering	1
MSc Engineering and Management	1
MSc International Hospitality Management	2
MSc Hospitality and Tourism Management	2
MA Communication Studies	2
MA Cultural Policy and Management	1
MA Industrial Design	1
MSc Networked Information Engineering	1
MSc Project Management	1

Table 2: The destination of summer 2000 Pre-Sessional students

Figure one shows the distribution of the Pre-Sessional exit test scores of the 38 Pre-Sessional students who continued on academic courses at SHU. It is interesting to note that 47% of the cohort had actually scored below 60 on the Pre-Sessional exit test and 53% had scored above. Given that there had been some scepticism expressed with regard to levels of language proficiency, it is interesting that, in fact, admissions tutors actually accepted a significant number of students who had gained results which were below the cut off point of 60%. This might suggest that they were putting some degree of confidence in the preparation for study at a UK university provided on the Pre-Sessional course.

Is English language proficiency the barrier to success?

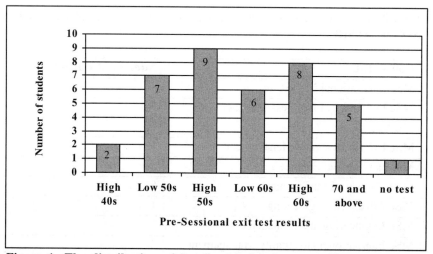

Figure 1: The distribution of Pre-Sessional exit test results amongst the cohort

The expected time for completion of Master's programmes at the University is December in the year after commencing the course. In December 2001, twenty (52%) of the above thirty eight students had passed their Master's courses. Table 3 shows their scores on the Pre-Sessional exit test.

Results on Pre-Sessional exit test	High 40s	Low 50s	High 50s	Low 60s	High 60s	70% and above	Did not take test
Numbers of students who had completed academic courses by December 2001	0	0	6	4	5	4	1
Numbers of students who had not completed academic courses by December 2001	2	7	3	2	3	1	0

Table 3: Pre-Sessional exit test scores of students in relation to Master's course completion in December 2001

This reveals that thirteen students who had passed their Master's courses at this point in time had achieved over 60% on their Pre-Sessional exit test. However, six students that had completed had scores in the high 50s on their exit test. This shows that if the score of 60 is taken as a rigid entry requirement, students who have the potential to succeed will be excluded. This accords with the findings of Allwright & Banerjee (1997) cited above in connection with IELTS scores which are just above or below Band 6.

From the data in Table 3, we can see that twelve students who had scored below 60 on their Pre-Sessional exit tests had not yet passed their courses but at the same time six students who did achieve 60 and above had not yet completed. In the same way as Allwright & Banerjee (1997) found in their study, in this research the results in the high 50s and low 60s do not predict whether students will pass or fail their academic courses. Some from each category had passed in December 2001 and some from each category had not.

These findings do not therefore reveal a clear-cut relationship between Pre-Sessional exit test scores and success or failure on academic courses. However, one clear observation that can be made is that students who had exit test results in the high 40s and low 50s were more likely to struggle on their courses and to have some referrals on their assignments. This had delayed their completion of the courses. It is significant that none of the students in these categories had passed their courses in December 2001 which suggests that their English language proficiency may have affected their ability to cope with the course.

Exit scores in the high 60s and above are more likely to result in a pass in the expected time on academic courses but do not completely guarantee it. Two students who had results in the high 60s on the Pre-Sessional exit test experienced referrals on their academic assignments and had not yet completed their academic courses in December 2001. Another student in this category had left for financial reasons although she had qualified to continue with her dissertation. The student who had achieved above 70% on the Pre-Sessional exit test was on track to complete by July 2002.It is therefore possible to say that these findings support those of Allwright & Banerjee who found that students must achieve IELTS 7.0 or above for there to be no risk at all of failure.

In March 2002, I did another trawl round the course administrators to investigate the progress of the 18 students shown in Table 3 who had not completed their academic courses in December 2001. Only one more student had completed his course. He had a Pre-Sessional exit test score of 46.5. This case stands out as unusual and does not support the hypothesis that there is a correlation between language proficiency on entry and successful course completion. The data shown in Table 4 is an amendment of that shown in Table 3 with the additional information highlighted.

Results on Pre-Sessional exit test	*High 40s*	Low 50s	High 50s	Low 60s	High 60s	70% and above	Did not take test
Numbers of students who had completed academic courses by March 2002	*1*	0	6	4	5	4	1
Numbers of students who had not completed academic courses by March 2002	0 + 1 left SHU	6 +1 left SHU	3	2	2 +1 left SHU	1	

Table 4: Pre-Sessional exit test scores of students in relation to Master's course completion in March 2002

Of the remaining 17 students who had not completed in March 2002, 14 had extensions for their Master's dissertations and were expected to complete in the summer of 2002. The Pre-Sessional exit scores of the 14 students who had extensions for their dissertations in March 2002 are shown above in Table 4. Although the number of students who scored below 60 on their Pre-Sessional exit test is greater than the number who scored above 60, the data does not reveal a clear correlation between language proficiency on entry and course completion in the predicted time.

As Tables 4 and 5 show, three students had left the university, one had failed her course, one had left for financial reasons despite completing the course work, and one had left within the first month of the course in October 2000. The exit scores of these three students are shown below in Table 5.

One cannot read too much from the small amount of data in Table 5 but it suggests an exit score in the low 50s could well signal problems for a student on their academic course if they are accepted. It also indicates that other circumstances intervene, which in the cases shown below were financial.

Nationality of student	Pre-Sessional exit test result	Reason for non-completion
Taiwanese	53.8	Failed course
Chinese	49.9	Left October 2000, possibly for financial reasons
Taiwanese	65.3	Left for financial reasons after successfully completing course work.

Table 5: Nationalities and Pre-Sessional exit test scores of students who had left the University

In July 2002, a further six students had completed their courses, therefore bringing the total to 27. In December 2002, the total reached 32 when an additional five had gained their awards. Three remaining students had extensions until early 2003. Table 6 shows the Pre-Sessional exit test scores of all the students who had completed by December 2002. Changes from Table 4 are indicated in brackets, thereby showing the Pre-Sessional exit test scores of the students completing their courses in July and December 2002.

Results on Pre-Sessional exit test	High 40s	Low 50s	High 50s	Low 60s	High 60s	70% and above	Did not take test
Numbers of students who had completed academic courses by December 2002	1	4 (+4)	8 (+2)	6 (+2)	7 (+2)	5 (+1)	1
Numbers of students who had not completed academic courses by December 2002	0	2	1	0	0	0	

Table 6: Pre-Sessional exit test scores of students in relation to Master's course completion in December 2002

Thus, in December 2002, 32 (84%) out of the total of 38 summer 2000 Pre-Sessional students had completed their academic courses. As mentioned above, three students had left the university without completing their courses. Three remaining students still had extensions until early 2003. Table 6 shows the Pre-Sessional exit test scores of this latter group.

As a summary of the results, Figure two presents a comparison of the time and number of completions of students who had achieved different Pre-Sessional exit test scores.

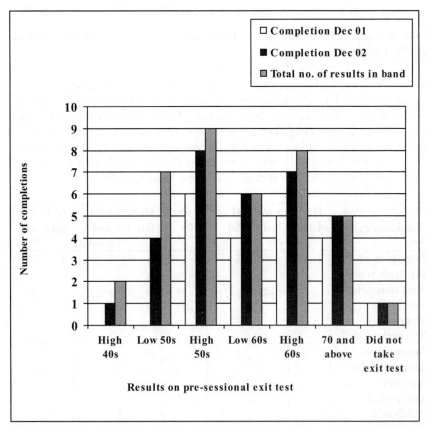

Figure two: A comparison of academic course completion rates at different times

Therefore, we can make the following significant observations from the data.

- There were no course completions in the expected time by students who had achieved below 55% on the Pre-Sessional exit test.
- The likelihood of academic course completion in the expected time by students who achieved in the high 50s and low 60s on the Pre-Sessional exit test was similar.
- There were still some students with Pre-Sessional exit test results above 60% who did not complete in the expected time.
- The three students who had still not completed but remained registered on their courses when the tracking finished in December 2002 had scored in the low 50s or high 50s on the Pre-Sessional exit test.

6. Conclusions

From these statistics, we can draw the conclusions below:

- The high percentage of students (84%) from the Pre-Sessional course who did complete their Master's course in the end indicates that the University does support students through the process once they have been accepted onto an academic course.
- One can speculate that the support they received on the Pre-Sessional course enabled students to succeed. They had developed study strategies which helped them despite achieving low results on the Pre-Sessional exit test.
- With regard to the question of the English language proficiency score / Pre-Sessional exit test result that is necessary to predict success on an academic course, it would appear that a cut off point of 60 for those that have completed the Pre-Sessional course would exclude students who have the potential to succeed. Students with exit test scores in the high 50s are no more likely to fall by the wayside or not complete in the expected time than students with scores in the low 60s. However, as academic tutors indicated in their quotes above, students in both these categories may struggle, particularly in the first semester, and this is where the enhancement of EAP support becomes crucial. Ongoing EAP support is essential to support students being accepted onto courses with scores just above or below 60% on the Pre-Sessional exit test.
- In connection with the actual testing procedure on the Pre-Sessional course, these findings suggest that the internal test provided for students serves as effective an indicator of likely student success as IELTS. The findings are very similar to those of Allwright & Banerjee

who used an IELTS score as their English language proficiency measure on entry. The Pre-Sessional exit test does appear to have predictive validity as those who achieved lower scores (i.e. below 55%) on the test took longer to complete their academic courses. This can serve as a reminder to academic departments that if they accept students with lower Pre-Sessional exit test results, they are likely to have to spend more time processing student assessments and to be willing to provide more individual support.

Notes:

There have been on-going developments in Pre-Sessional provision and the Pre-Sessional exit test at SHU since the initial research was undertaken in 2000-2002. In particular, the reporting of students' levels to academic departments is currently under discussion with a proposal to move towards broader bandings which incorporate a list of statements indicating what students have shown they can do in an academic context (Banerjee & Wall, 2006). Sheffield Hallam University continues to offer free In-Sessional English language and study skills support for all international students.

The research report on which this paper is based is available as a pdf document. If you would like to obtain a copy, please email Diana Ridley at d.m.ridley@sheffield.ac.uk

References

Allwright, J. & Banerjee, J. (1997). Investigating the accuracy of admissions criteria: a case study in a British University. In C. Clapham & D. Wall, (Eds.), *Language Testing Update, 22*. Lancaster: International Language Testing Association Official Newsletter

Banerjee, J. & Wall, D. (2006). Assessing and reporting performances on Pre-Sessional EAP courses: Developing a final assessment checklist and investigating its validity. *Journal of English for Academic Purposes, 5*, 50-69.

Meldrum, G. (1996). Towards the revision of an assessment and banding procedure by way of a criterion-related study. In M. Hewings & T. Dudley-Evans (Eds.), *Evaluation and course design in EAP* (Review of English Language Teaching 6(1), 15-25). Hemel Hempstead: Prentice Hall MacMillan in association with the British Council.

Moore, T. & Morton, J. (2005). Dimensions of difference: A comparison of university writing and IELTS writing. *Journal of English for Academic Purposes, 4,* 43-66.

Ridley, D. (2002). *Tracking the experiences and progress of a cohort of TESOL Centre Pre-Sessional students: Implications for support and language proficiency on entry.* Sheffield Hallam University: Research Report.

Ridley, D. (2004). Puzzling experiences in higher education: critical moments for conversation. *Studies in Higher Education, 29,* 91-107.

Tonkyn, A. (1995). English language proficiency standards for overseas students: Who needs what level? *Journal of International Education, 6,* 37-61.

Tracking Pre-Sessional students' writing abilities at the University of Hertfordshire

Mary Martala, University of Hertfordshire

Abstract

This paper offers the results of a case study which attempted to assess the effectiveness of the writing component of the University of Hertfordshire's 3-month Pre-Sessional course. The aim of the case study was to identify whether the writing strand equips Chinese students at postgraduate level with the academic writing skills they will need in their subsequent Master's degree courses. The study took into consideration both relevant literature and students' own perceptions and writing data.

Evidence from students' written data and answers to feedback questionnaires seem to indicate that students had been well prepared by the writing input and practice provided by the Pre-Sessional course. The results further suggest that students' attitudes to study had a major effect on their success.

1. Introduction

Academic writing is critical to the success of students studying in British higher education as the assessment processes predominantly involve written assignments and examinations. British students are generally introduced to academic writing in the latter part of their high school education. This is then further developed in their undergraduate study. International students, however, may not have this experience, particularly in English, yet they often come to the UK for further studies with knowledge of their own culture's education system. The differences which exist between the various systems of education often create a gap in students' knowledge of the assessment processes and thus academic writing expectations. This knowledge gap coupled with an inadequate linguistic level invariably affects student performance.

In order to study in the UK students attend preparatory courses which aim to improve their language skills and cultural knowledge of their target country of study. To date, preparatory courses for study in the UK are mainly aimed at helping students pass the IELTS examination. International students can typically gain direct entry to a University in the UK with an IELTS mark of between 6 and 7. Although the IELTS exam mark indicates the students' competence in English, students are found not to have the necessary skills to cope with the type of academic assessment they will encounter on their degree courses. As a result, preparatory courses within UK Higher Education institutions have been operating for over a decade with the aim of improving both the linguistic capabilities of the students and their knowledge of the assessment processes thus bridging the gap mentioned earlier. These courses are often termed Foundation, Bridging or Pre-Master's and Pre-Sessional.

At the University of Hertfordshire, the Pre-Sessional courses are run in the summer for a period of 1 – 3 months. Once the students have fulfilled the criteria for entering into these preparatory courses, the responsibility lies with the English department to ensure that a syllabus which will equip students with the necessary skills to partake in their under/postgraduate courses will be provided. The syllabus at the University of Hertfordshire has been designed to cater for any nationality; nevertheless, as students attending these courses are predominantly Chinese, certain assumptions have been made regarding the way these students have been taught in China. These assumptions, based on experience of teaching Chinese students and published material, include the concepts that the students are not encouraged to critically evaluate information, that the ideas provided in books are usually memorised for later use, that copying from sources without providing references is acceptable and that the writing of an essay should allow the reader to infer information which results in the writing of non-explicit text (Belcher & Braine, 1995; Jin & Cortazzi, 1996; Mohan & Lo, 1985). An interest in seeing to what extent the University of Hertfordshire Pre-Sessional course prepared students for their further studies and whether these culturally based assumptions were true prompted this research.

In an attempt to answer these questions, this study made use of published material which looked at the significance of and approaches to the teaching of academic writing at a UK Higher Education institution. Three approaches were considered, namely 'the product approach' (Badger & White, 2000; White 1988), 'the process approach' (Coffin, Curry, Goodman, Hewings, Lillis & Swann, 2003; Curry & Hewings, 2003; Dudley-Evans, 1995; Turk & Kirkham, 1992), and 'the genre approach' (Badger & White, 2000; Thompson, 2000; Weissberg & Buker, 1990). In addition, areas which may impede in the teaching of writing were examined, such as diverse expectations of students' writing by different faculties (Braine, 1995; Hartley & Chesworth, 1999; Lea & Street, 1998; Leki, 1995; Weir, 1988) and tutor feedback (Atherton, 2000; Curry & Hewings, 2003; Ferris, 2001; Pallant, 2000). The role of the learner was then considered before specifically looking at some of the problems Chinese students encounter with academic writing in a second language such as linguistic ability, cultural background, and issues of plagiarism (Biggs & Watkins, 1999; Blue, 2000; Cotterall, 2000; Goodman & Swann, 2003; Green, 2000; Jin & Cortazzi, 1996; Little, 1999; Mohan & Lo, 1985; Richards, 2000; Woodward-Kron, 2002). It was beyond the scope of this paper to give details of the published theories. However, the references above include the relevant material.

International students invest a great deal of time and money into obtaining a degree from a British institution. Ensuring that our preparatory programmes are effective in helping these students attain their goals is vital. The case study makes an initial attempt to evaluate the writing component of one such programme. This work examines postgraduate Chinese students' writing experience prior to the Pre-Sessional three-month course. It then attempts to gauge what the students perceive to be learning as opposed to what they are actually learning during the course. This is achieved by comparing students' responses to four questionnaires with evidence provided in their writing of six essays. A fifth questionnaire seeks the students' evaluation of the Pre-Sessional course after their first semester on their degree course. Two essays from the students' work in the first semester are also assessed in terms of the effectiveness of the Pre-Sessional programme. Results and tentative conclusions are presented.

2. Background information on the study

2.1. The setting

The University of Hertfordshire has been established for 13 years. The University operates from three campuses, and currently teaches 22,000 students, over 10% of whom are international fee payers. The last 11 years has seen a steady growth in international student numbers from a wide-ranging cultural background. Approximately 50% are currently from China.

International students enter the University either through direct entry or through progression from preparatory programmes. The English Language Teaching Unit, operating within the School of Combined Studies, offers four such programmes all of which place emphasis on the study skills required for university study in conjunction with improving English language ability. This study focuses on the three-month Pre-Sessional programme as taught in the period July to September 2004.

2.2. The programme

The Pre-Sessional programme (run in the summer period and varying in length between one, two, and three months) prepares students for entry to either a graduate or a postgraduate degree. Its aims are to improve students' command of English to an equivalent of a 6 or 6.5 on the IELTS scale, develop their English for academic purposes, and develop their study skills. The assessment is 100% exam-based.

In the Pre-Sessional programme students are grouped according to whether they will follow an undergraduate or a postgraduate programme and wherever possible according to the subject they will study, in order to maximise the use of the in-class materials. The programme requires 21 hours of contact time per week and allows for 9 hours of private study. The tutor-led sessions are divided into seven classes of reading, listening, speaking, project (x 2 classes), writing, and general English. Each class is based on a Definitive Module Document (DMD) which describes the aims of the sessions. In order for these aims to be fulfilled, detailed material and briefing sheets are offered to tutors, which include records of work, assignment titles, marking criteria and feedback forms. A staff briefing session is arranged in advance of each course and there are weekly tutor meetings for questions and updates.

2.3. The teachers

The teachers working on the Pre-Sessional programme are qualified to a minimum of a Certificate standard with five years' teaching experience. Most of the teachers have also attained Diploma standard and a growing number have a Master's degree. The teachers have a solid EAP teaching background with extensive experience in EFL, ESOL or ESP.

2.4. The subjects

The subjects of this study are 7 East Asian female postgraduate students, ranging from 24 to 28 years of age. Postgraduate students were targeted for this study as the researcher wanted to ascertain to what extent students were taught academic writing at undergraduate level in China and how it compared with practices in the UK. Five of the students are from China and the remaining two are from Taiwan. All students had completed 4-year Bachelor degrees and achieved at least IELTS 5.5 or equivalent on entry. These students were not specifically targeted (other than for being graduates). The researcher was their allocated writing teacher at the start of the programme. All students have since completed postgraduate programmes at the Business School at the University of Hertfordshire.

2.5. Course content

The content of the writing component of the Pre-Sessional course was decided upon by considering the types of assignments the students would be required to undertake in their postgraduate studies as well as the organisation style, academic language and referencing rules which they would be expected to adhere to. To this end, one course book was chosen which seemed to cater both for the needs of the students and their future degree subject tutors. This course book was *Academic Writing* by Steven Bailey, (published in London in 2003 by RoutledgeFalmer) and it was to be used throughout the Pre-Sessional programme. Only two thirds of the units were covered as it was felt they provided the necessary basis for the students' future studies. Units included comparing essay to report writing; producing a plan; organising ideas into paragraphs taking cohesion and use of impersonal writing into consideration; writing introductions and conclusions; avoiding plagiarism through use of summary, paraphrase and appropriate referencing; improving the overall writing style of the students through use of cohesive markers and conjunctions, and knowledge of formal and informal language.

The course was therefore aimed at providing students with the knowledge and skills they would need to succeed in their future degrees.

2.6. Assessment

As one of the main purposes of academic writing is for assessment, naturally, students' writing was frequently assessed. The students were required to write two essays per month as course work and one further essay as part of the "exit test" at the end of each Pre-Sessional month. This was to ascertain whether the students were meeting the required standard as set out in the marking criteria. In each Pre-Sessional course one of the two essays was administered in class to provide practice of test conditions. Promoting reflection in the students' work was apparent in the choice of essay titles. Essays would typically include elements taught during the course such as ability to write introductions or summarise the main points, in addition to asking students to reflect on what they have learnt and how it has helped them fulfil the requirements of the set task.

Essays were assessed using detailed criteria in an attempt to standardise marking.

Following the marking of the essays, the EAP teachers provided written feedback to the students on the marking profiles they had completed. It was then left to each teacher's discretion and class time availability to decide whether oral feedback would also be given on a tutorial basis.

3. Description of the study

Chinese postgraduate students were chosen for this study mainly because they represented the highest number of non-native speaker students at the University of Hertfordshire. The study intended to seek answers to three questions described as aims below.

The first aim was to ascertain to what degree the students were able to meet the expectations of the writing component. An analysis of the requirements of the course needed to be matched to the students' written work (essays) to fulfil this aim as well as an evaluation of the students' own observations which were sought through questionnaires.

The second aim was to assess the students' perceptions of the writing course and the extent to which the course helped them during the early stages of their degree. Student feedback sought through additional questionnaires was paramount in accomplishing this aim in addition to further evidence of students' writing whilst on their degrees.

The final aim was to assess to what degree Chinese students were being taught new techniques in a UK academic setting. Use of questionnaires was equally important in realising this aim.

The study was carried out over a three-month period starting in June 2004 with further student contact in February 2005. Postgraduate students were selected for this study as it was assumed that they would have been exposed to writing practice on their undergraduate degree programmes and the researcher was interested in an underlying comparison of text types and procedures used in China as opposed to the UK. The class to which the researcher was appointed as writing teacher formed the research group. The researcher was their writing tutor throughout the Pre-Sessional programme as this would facilitate maintaining contact with the students both during the summer and whilst on their degrees.

Each of the students completed a total of five questionnaires to aid this study. The questionnaires were used as a means of gauging students' previous experience; gaining an insight into course expectations; gathering course feedback; and testing students' learning. The first questionnaire was given to students at the beginning of their Pre-Sessional course in order to ascertain their previous writing experience. Questionnaires 2, 3 and 4 were given at the end of each month of study in order to assess the students' perceptions of what they were learning. The final questionnaire asked students to rate the Pre-Sessional course in light of their experience as Master's degree students. The questionnaires were designed to make direct reference to material taught in any one month. Students in effect were asked to state what they had learned; to evaluate the usefulness of the taught material; and to reflect on their own learning and progress.

Students were expected to provide answers both through closed and through open-ended questions. Students were asked to tick one or more relevant box(es); provide answers to questions; and supply further details to support answers to closed questions.

In addition to the questionnaires, the students were asked to present their written work for analysis. This was in the form of essays which they completed as part of their three-month Pre-Sessional course. By comparing the student answers to the questionnaires with examples of their written work it could be seen to what extent the students' reflections matched their practice. The comparison would offer a good indication of whether what they *perceived* to be learning was equivalent to what they were *actually* learning. The essays would also provide evidence of whether the course requirements were being achieved and whether they were therefore realistic. Combining the answers from the questionnaires to the essay comments would further provide an indication of whether students were acquiring new skills and practices with which they could experiment in their essay writing or whether skills learned in their home country could be transferred to a UK academic setting.

Two further samples were taken from the students' assessed work in Semester A in order to observe how students fared on their degree courses.

4. How the information was used for analysis

The answers to the questionnaires were grouped according to similarity of response for the open-ended questions, and as the closed questions were easier to quantify, tables were drawn showing students' responses. Where responses varied greatly, students' actual answers were noted. Pseudonyms were used.

Students' individual essays were then analysed and information was divided into three areas. The first area described the points which were taught prior to the setting of each essay; the second area identified the strengths of each student's essay and whether use of items taught is salient; and the final area classified the weaknesses and the points which required further attention for improvement to be made.

The essay data was then compared to the students' answers to the questionnaires thus enabling the researcher to gauge what students perceived to be learning as opposed to what they were actually learning as well as the students' overall ability to reflect.

Different analysis was used for the students' subject specific essays. The marking criteria used by the subject tutors were unknown, therefore the points considered for the purposes of the study were criteria similar to those of the Pre-Sessional course in addition to the comments made by the tutors and an overall impression gained by reading the students' work.

5. Results and discussion

This section focuses on the findings of the case study starting with an examination of the students' answers to the questionnaires and followed by an analysis of their coursework essays and their degree assignments. It must be noted that the findings of the questionnaires cannot alone offer a sufficient account of the course content. It is only in comparison with the students' essays that a more representative picture emerges. Equally, the small scale of this study can merely be viewed as a stepping-stone to further research which can be carried out on a much larger scale.

5.1. The questionnaires

The initial questionnaire concentrated on students' previous experience, specifically students' exposure to different writing genres & academic writing conventions and students' referencing practices.

The results indicated that all students had had previous exposure in writing essays/reports whilst at university in their home towns with titles and essay models provided by the tutor. There was varied understanding both of the process of organising an essay and of referencing techniques, though most students had written essays by combining authors' ideas with theirs or using authors' ideas to support theirs.

The second questionnaire attempted to gauge whether students were acquiring new skills and whether they were able to identify them as well as their general feelings. It further attempted to see if there was a difference in taught writing techniques between the UK and their home country.

The results showed that essay organisation, planning and writing conclusions were skills identified as new and the students felt interested by the lesson content though some were "accepting" at having to learn something new. No clear differences between the countries were cited.

The third questionnaire checked whether students were learning and whether they were aware of necessary techniques for successful writing. It was also an opportunity to see if classes covered what the students had expected and what they would wish to study in the next Pre-Sessional.

The results demonstrated confusion over paraphrase, summary and synthesis despite students having a clear understanding of their future use. An awareness of the importance of planning, re-reading, re-writing, editing, proofreading and checking tutor feedback was shown but students admitted to not always editing sufficiently. Students had expected teacher correction, grammar, games and easier ways of writing essays and they asked for future classes in grammar, vocabulary, cohesive markers, and differences between formal and informal styles.

In the fourth questionnaire students were asked if they felt prepared for their degree course, and if they would recommend the Pre-Sessional course.

The students' answers showed that the majority of students lacked confidence despite admitting their writing ability had improved. Poor grammar skills, insufficient vocabulary and difficulty in organising an essay were cited as worries. With the exception of one student, all the others would recommend the Pre-Sessional course.

The fifth questionnaire asked for essay results from the first semester of the students' degree course and lecturer feedback as well as retrospective feedback on the Pre-Sessional course.

The students' grades did not point to progressive improvement and there were four instances of language related problems indicated by tutor feedback. The Pre-Sessional course was rated from very useful to adequate with students suggesting essay models and further work on referencing for future courses.

The small scale of the research and the impossible task of evaluating external conditions for students' individual learning (time spent reinforcing coursework; interaction with native speakers, and other factors) does not allow for any conclusive remarks as to the effect of the Pre-Sessional course on the students' success in their postgraduate studies. Nevertheless, the students' impressions of the three-month course seem to confirm that the content was highly relevant to their needs, which is all that can be expected.

This section has sought to provide the research findings based on the devised questionnaires whilst also acknowledging certain limitations. The following section which analyses the students' actual written work is essential for a more holistic view of the meaning of these results.

5.2. The essays

An analysis of the six 500-word essays written during the Pre-Sessional course and of two written assignments from the first semester of the students' degree study was made.

The essay writing part of this study focused on each student individually and attempted to assess the knowledge they gained and the progress they made throughout the three months. References to the student questionnaires were made in an attempt to match the students' perceptions to the actual findings. The extent to which the tutor feedback was utilised by the students was also examined in addition to the students' ability to reflect on their learning. Due to the scope of this paper, only three of the students are exemplified, though the concluding section encompasses all results.

Student 1 - Anna

Anna was previously taught essay writing through models and from the start she did not show any major problems with sentence structure. Her use of formal language developed well and she also responded positively to feedback. She was able to perceive newly acquired skills but her development of referencing though accurate remained inconsistent. Her degree work was of an excellent standard overall achieving marks of mainly As and Bs.

Student 2 - Sarah

Sarah's writing included fairly good use of grammar and vocabulary but she needed practice in academic language as she tended to overuse informal words. Her essay organisation needed improvement but her response to feedback was fairly good. She showed good reflection on her learning as well as accurate reflection of areas to improve. Sarah progressed well overall. She improved on the required areas and despite some errors in structure, which were not commented on by subject tutors, she produced constant degree work in the range of 50-59%. It was pleasing to note in her final questionnaire that she viewed "writing" as her strength.

Student 3 - Dianne

Dianne's vocabulary was limited and informal at the start of the course. She made errors in language use and had problems with organisation. Though the latter improved, Dianne showed limited understanding of her own progress. The inaccuracy and informality in her work continued and there was some confusion over in-text referencing. Dianne responded to tutor feedback given in the Pre-Sessional at some point during Semester A. The subject tutors did not penalise her apparent weakness in grammar skills and her Semester A results consisted of 2 Cs, 3 Bs and 1 A.

Pre-Sessional course essay findings indicated that *some* students struggled with language use, academic vocabulary, essay organisation, motivation and lack of response to tutor feedback and that *all* students had problems with referencing to different degrees throughout the course.

Master's degree course essay findings revealed that lack of critical analysis was an issue for two students and that there were some language related problems. However, there were no referencing issues.

At this point, it is important to consider to what extent the following four areas may have affected student results:

1. Linguistic ability
2. Cultural background
3. Tutor feedback
4. Learner attitude

On the subject of linguistic ability, the Pre-Sessional course seems to have the pass mark at the right level. All the students who passed the Pre-Sessional course succeeded in obtaining their Master's degree. Nevertheless, the linguistic ability required on degree courses seems highly dependent on the degree subjects being studied and on the tutors marking the work.

In the area of cultural background, there is evidence of an element of the reproductive approach. All students had previously been taught through models and they now found themselves in the UK being expected to "critically evaluate" with insufficient understanding of the term. Model essays were asked for, the students saw teachers as figures of authority and there was a reluctance to ask questions in class, examples which are in keeping with their Chinese background.

Tutor feedback was utilised in varying degrees. In some cases immediate improvement was shown, in others improvement with word/sentence corrections seemed easier to respond to than organisation, and in a few cases, improvement did not become evident until Semester A. There is a need for further research in the area of tutor feedback and its role in student learning.

The final area to be considered is learners' attitude to study. This was analysed by combining answers to questionnaires with their behaviour in class in addition to gauging their response to tutor feedback on assignments and monitoring their development of writing.

Results of the analysis indicated that there was a strong correlation between students' attitudes to study and improvement in their writing skills. Students seemed to make slower progress when they did not respond to feedback, when they did not ask questions in class and when they could not identify their own problem areas. There is therefore some evidence to suggest that there is a strong correlation between students' attitudes to study and their assessment results as displayed in the table below. Students' attitude is measured on a scale of 1 – 5 with 1 being the most positive indicator. Looking at the grade point average (where the lower the grade the better the performance) it seems that with one sole exception, the performance grade strongly correlates with the attitude grade. Unquestionably, the exception coupled with the low scale of this study requires there to be further research into attitudes and performance.

	Entry	Exit	GPA	Attitude
Anna	50	60	5	1
Jasmine	52	56	6.8	5
Margaret	63	55	7.8	1
Dinah	53	53	9.2	4
Sarah	45	52	10.5	5
Dianne	44	50	8.7	3
Mary	52	45	8.8	4

Table 1: Analysis of student performance

6. Conclusion

The case study described in this paper has attempted to evaluate the effectiveness of the writing element of the Pre-Sessional course in enabling Chinese students to follow a postgraduate programme at the University of Hertfordshire. The study has taken into consideration both relevant literature and students' own perceptions and writing data and the following conclusions have been reached.

The writing component of the three-month Pre-Sessional programme at the University of Hertfordshire makes use of a number of recognised methods and approaches in its syllabus design. Elements of the process approach are utilised in terms of essay planning and drafting. These are supported by elements of the genre approach in terms of raising awareness of the purpose for the writing. Student autonomy is valued and encouraged and to this end essay titles are created which enable students to reflect on their learning. The actual course content focuses on the skills which students will need on their degree courses concentrating on areas such as organisation of ideas, use of appropriate academic vocabulary and methods of incorporating material from other sources.

The students who participated in this study were able to meet the expectations of the writing component by passing all the course work with varying degrees of success. Their perceptions of the course were mainly positive and they seemed to be learning completely new skills as well as skills which only required small adaptations of their previous learning experience. Results of the students' work in Semester A confirm that the majority of the students were meeting the assignment criteria set by their subject tutors. This further seems to confirm that the writing input and practice provided by the Pre-Sessional course helped the students cope with work given to them by their tutors. There is therefore evidence to suggest that English for Academic Purposes classes enable students to succeed, as students who passed the Pre-Sessional course also passed their degree.

The study further puts forward a reasonable assumption that students' attitude to study has a major effect on their educational success. The results seem to point to two issues which future research could address, namely analysis of attitude-related performance and assessment of the benefit of student feedback.

References

Atherton, B. (2000). Developing accuracy in academic writing. In G. M. Blue, J. Milton & J. Saville (Eds.), *Assessing English for academic purposes* (pp. 259-269). Oxford: Peter Lang.

Badger, R. & White, G. (2000). A process genre approach to teaching writing. *ELT Journal, 54,* 153-160.

Belcher, D. & Braine, G. (Eds.). (1995). *Academic writing in a second language: Essays on research and pedagogy.* Norwood, NJ: Ablex.

Biggs, J. B. & Watkins, D. A. (1999). The Chinese learner in retrospect. In D. A. Watkins & J. B. Biggs (Eds.), *The Chinese learner: Cultural, psychological and contextual influences* (pp. 269-285). Hong Kong: Comparative Education Research Centre, University of Hong Kong.

Blue, G. M. (2000). Self-assessment and defining learners' needs. In G. M. Blue, J. Milton & J. Saville (Eds.), *Assessing English for academic purposes* (pp. 237-255). Oxford: Peter Lang.

Braine, G. (1995). Writing in the natural sciences and engineering. In D. Belcher & G. Braine (Eds.). (1995). *Academic writing in a second language: Essays on research and pedagogy* (pp. 113 – 134). Norwood, NJ: Ablex.

Coffin, C., Curry, M. J., Goodman, S., Hewings, A., Lillis, T. M. & Swann, J. (2003). *Teaching academic writing: A toolkit for higher education.* London: Routledge.

Cotterall, S. (2002). Promoting learner autonomy through the curriculum: Principles for designing language courses. *ELT Journal, 54*, 109-117.

Curry, M. J. & Hewings, A. (2003). Approaches to teaching writing. In Coffin, C., Curry, M. J., Goodman, S., Hewings, A., Lillis, T. M. & Swann, J. (2003). *Teaching academic writing: A toolkit for higher education* (pp19-44). London: Routledge.

Dudley-Evans, T. (1995). Common-core and specific approaches to the teaching of academic writing. In D. Belcher & G. Braine (Eds.), *Academic writing in a second language* (pp. 293-312). Norwood, NJ: Ablex.

Ferris, D. R. (2001). Teaching writing for academic purposes. In J. Flowerdew & M. Peacock (Eds.), *Research perspectives on English for academic purposes* (pp. 298-314). Cambridge: Cambridge University Press.

Goodman, S. & Swann, J. (2003). Planning the assessment of student writing. In Coffin, C., Curry, M. J., Goodman, S., Hewings, A., Lillis, T. M. & Swann, J. (2003). *Teaching academic writing: A toolkit for higher education* (pp73-100). London: Routledge.

Green, R. (2000). Life after the Pre-Sessional course: How students fare in their departments. In G. M. Blue, J. Milton & J. Saville (Eds.), *Assessing English for academic purposes* (pp. 131-145). Oxford: Peter Lang.

Hartley, J. & Chesworth, K. (1999). What difficulties do first-year university students find in essay writing? Some results from a questionnaire study. In P. Thompson, (Ed.), *Academic writing development in higher education: Perspectives, explorations and approaches* (pp. 62-72). Reading: Centre for Applied Language Studies, University of Reading.

Jin, L. & Cortazzi, M. (1996). 'This way is very different from Chinese ways': EAP needs and academic culture. In M. Hewings and T. Dudley-Evans (Eds.), *Evaluation and course design in EAP* (pp. 205-216). Hemel Hempstead: Phoenix.

Lea, M. R. & Street, B. V. (1998). Student writing in higher education: An academic literacies approach. *Studies in Higher Education, 23,* 157-172.

Leki, I. (1995). Good writing: I know it when I see it. In D. Belcher & G. Braine (Eds.), *Academic writing in a second language: Essays on research and pedagogy* (pp. 23 – 46). Norwood, NJ: Ablex.

Little, D. (1999). *Learner autonomy 1: Definitions, issues and problems.* Dublin: Authentik Language Learning Resources Ltd.

Mohan, B. A. & Lo, W. A-Y. (1985). Academic writing and Chinese students: Transfer and development factors. *TESOL Quarterly, 19,* 515-34.

Pallant, A. (2000). Developing critical thinking in writing. In P. Thompson, (Ed.), *Patterns and perspectives: Insights into EAP writing practice* (pp. 103 – 116). Reading: Centre for Applied Language Studies, University of Reading.

Richards, R. (2000). How does the development of critical thinking relate to the demands of academic writing in higher education? In P. Thompson, (Ed.), *Patterns and perspectives: Insights into EAP writing practice* (pp. 88 – 102). Reading: Centre for Applied Language Studies, University of Reading.

Thompson, P. (Ed.). (2000). *Patterns and perspectives: Insights into EAP writing practice.* Reading: Centre for Applied Language Studies, University of Reading.

Turk, C. & Kirkham, J. (1992). *Effective writing* (2nd ed.). London: E. & F. N. Spon.

Wall, D., Nickson, A., Jordan, R., Allwright J., Houghton, D. (1988). Developing student writing – a subject tutor and writing tutors compare points of view. In Robinson, P. (Ed.). *Academic writing: Process and product* (ELT Documents, 129, pp.117 – 129). London: Modern English Publications.

Weir, C. (1988). Academic writing – can we please all the people all the time? In P. Robinson (Ed.), *Academic writing: Process and product* (ELT Documents, 129, pp.17– 34). London: Modern English Publications.

Weissberg, R. & Buker, S. (1990). *Writing up research: Experimental research report writing for students of English.* Englewood Cliffs, NJ: Prentice Hall Regents.

White, R. (1988). Academic writing: Process and product. In P. Robinson (Ed.). *Academic writing: Process and product* (ELT Documents, 129, pp.4 – 16). London: Modern English Publications.

Woodward-Kron, R. (2002). Critical analysis versus description? Examining the relationship in successful student writing. *Journal of English for Academic Purposes, 1,* 121-143.

Mainland Chinese postgraduate students during their Master's dissertations: Some reflections and thoughts on the effectiveness of EAP from the students' perspective

Nick Pilcher, Heriot-Watt University, Edinburgh

Abstract

There has been growing demand in the field of EAP for concrete studies on the effectiveness of EAP and although some studies have begun to emerge to date, the findings have often been more in the form of claims to success rather than evidence of success. The conclusions have provided confirmation for EAP tutors rather than hard facts for Chancellors. Although this paper does not claim to provide hard facts for Chancellors, it hopes to provide some feedback to EAP tutors in the form of students' perceptions of the effectiveness of their EAP courses while undertaking their Master's Dissertations. The paper reports comments from a group of 21 students from Mainland China who were doing Postgraduate dissertations at Heriot-Watt University in the summer of 2005. It concludes that overall there were more positive comments about EAP than negative although the picture is an extremely complex one. It also reports some challenges for EAP that arise from some of the participants' comments and reports on data that supports the need for EAP. The paper concludes that although the initial data is generally supportive of EAP there is a need to gather more data in this area. It also advocates more links between EAP tutors and departments, not only to help gather this data but to further develop the effectiveness of EAP provision and support.

1. Introduction

This paper summarises and provides a rather more complete picture of the poster presented on my behalf at the BALEAP Professional Issues Meeting at Hertfordshire in June 2006 by Olwyn Alexander. It briefly describes the context, purpose and methodology of the research and then gives some key results from the data that it is hoped will be of use both to EAP tutors in preparing EAP courses and also for EAP course directors. It is hoped that for EAP course directors where the data is positive it will be of use in promoting EAP provision across the University and where the data is negative it will be of use in feeding back into the EAP courses where deemed appropriate or possible.

2. Context and purpose of the research

Within most postgraduate education writing plays a major role in the form of assessment, through written assignments, exams and dissertations. Students from China often experience difficulty both at a macro and a micro level with managing and producing written discourse in these forms in English (Kirkpatrick, 2004). It is the aim of many EAP courses to help ameliorate these difficulties by providing Pre-Sessional support that is designed to prepare students for what they will encounter on their degree programmes, both in building upon their knowledge of Academic English and in raising their awareness of previously unfamiliar UK academic practices such as report formats and the importance of correct citation of others' work.

At Heriot-Watt University a number of students follow a BALEAP accredited EAP 12 week summer Pre-Sessional course (and / or a Heriot-Watt University accredited year round Pre-Sessional course[1]) that includes both of the aims mentioned above. Research into EAP has investigated the perceptions of students immediately after their EAP Pre-Sessionals (Banerjee & Wall, 2006) and how results and findings from degree programmes should feed back into EAP (Allison, 2004). Research into EAP has also investigated the relevance of EAP (Harwood, 2005; Hyland & Hamp-Lyons, 2002) through a contrast with other English for General Purposes courses such as IELTS (Moore & Morton, 2005) and it has investigated difficulties encountered by second language students during their courses (Bitchener & Basturkmen, 2006).

Yet there has been little research into the effectiveness of EAP from the perspective of students on their courses. Some research has found the vocabulary knowledge of students promoted to their degrees from an EAP course as opposed to those placed directly on their degrees to have been lower (Clark & Ishida, 2005), and that these promoted students' ability to acquire general and academic vocabulary throughout a subsequent advanced reading course was actually lower than that of the placed students. This is in spite of the fact that the promoted students had taken a semester of study in an EAP programme (Clark & Ishida, 2005). Indeed, it is suggested here that one possible reason for the lack of research is due to a wariness that the results could be unflattering for EAP, as well as the relatively young nature of the field and the potential difficulties with collecting data such as access to students and staff and the constraints of time.

The data presented here comes from interviews with a number of Mainland Chinese students during their Master's dissertations. The interviews form part of the data for a larger study the author is undertaking to investigate mainland Chinese students' experiences during their Master's dissertations and comparing these with the thoughts of the departmental supervisors. This larger study is mentioned here as it explains why in the results section below some of the comments from the participants were unsolicited and some were solicited. A number of the students interviewed had followed some or all of the Pre-

Sessional course at Heriot-Watt university. It is one of the aims of the larger study that their perceptions will provide useful perspectives on the EAP course that could be used to provide constructive feedback for tutors on the EAP Pre-Sessional at Heriot-Watt University and for the larger EAP community.

3. Methodology

The data was gathered using interviews of around 40 minutes each. These were semi structured (Cohen & Manion, 1994) to allow for less rigidity, 'respondent' centred (Powney & Watts, 1987) in that they were mostly guided by the interviewer (as opposed to interviewee guided 'informant' interviews) and 'active' (Gubrium & Holstein, 2000) in that points of interest were pursued and participants encouraged to ask questions of the interviewer.

The students (hereafter referred to as participants where the author is referring to those who took part in the study, and students where the author is referring to students generally) were interviewed at four points during the dissertation, once as close to the start of the dissertation as possible, secondly after they had been studying and reading for four weeks, thirdly when they were near completion and fourthly after they had handed in their dissertation. Twenty one participants were interviewed initially, and then eighteen participants who were able to continue, and data was collected from them for the remaining three interviews. They were interviewed iteratively and were asked questions about the difficulties they were experiencing, what they thought a good dissertation was, and other issues (a list of the initial questions is in appendix A).

Questions about the success of the EAP programme were not asked specifically in the list of questions, rather, the interviewer waited for any comments to arise naturally and if they did not, asked the participants their thoughts about the EAP course at some point during the interviews. This was designed to avoid as far as possible 'good' subjects giving responses they considered helpful and 'apprehensive' subjects being reluctant to make unpopular responses (Bochner, 1980; Crowne & Marlowe, 1964; Orne, 1962, 1970). The interviews were transcribed using a self-generated coding system (Silverman, 2000) and analysed phenomenologically (Hycner, 1999) by 'distilling' the data into manageable chunks and grouping points with similar relevance.

4. Results and discussion

Of the twenty one participants who were interviewed at the start of the study, eleven had followed EAP courses or Undergraduate study in the UK. Of the eighteen participants who continued nine had taken EAP courses or

Undergraduate study in the UK. The results refer to these throughout and are divided into three sections A: Evidence for EAP; B: Challenges for EAP; C: The Need for EAP.

4.1. Section A: Evidence for EAP

4.1.1. Unsolicited references to English courses

Three participants mentioned their EAP Pre-Sessional course at Heriot-Watt as having been useful in helping them with their dissertation, pointing out that

> *from experience of my er during my studying English I think er it's enough to carry out dissertation* (CS[2]),

and another participant mentioned a combination of having done the EAP Pre-Sessional and help in the department, saying that

> *because I I have already learnt from the language school the demonstrate for the project and also yesterday the writing lectures so I know the abstracts and the body and the summary* (AS).

Another participant pointed out that

> *I think it's the same er Foundation English about er writing the dissertation* (CS),

and this participant said that the Pre-Sessional had also helped with the course work, in that

> *this coursework is like the project* (on the EAP Pre-Sessional) (CS).

Similarly, another participant said that they thought the Pre-Sessional had been

> *useful for me at the beginning because I know I think I have improved myself in the academic in this year and the the main dissertation is something different and more difficult than what I do in last year in the summer course* (CS).

In reference to courses elsewhere, another participant spoke of an EAP course they had done elsewhere:

> *for 6 months listening, writing, especially writing the essay writing the dissertation giving out presentation so I was kind of prepared* (AS).

One participant spoke of their regret at not doing an English course:

> *I haven't read the, take the language course in UK I graduate then I come here so I don't know how to write er dissertation in English ... I only only take TOEFL test but I think it's not enough* (CS).

Similarly, another said that the English course they had done was not of much use as they had not done EAP:

> *it's not that useful ... I think two months I think it's no (pause) we never study stuff like quotes And we during that course the teacher set very easy questions erm just give you a chance to talk in English* (AS).

Overall these comments indicate that these participants found the EAP courses they had done useful although one participant commented on the difference in scale of what they were now doing. Also corroborating this is how little use two of the participants said they got out of English for General Purposes or the TOEFL exam preparation course.

4.1.2. Solicited references to English courses

A number of participants were asked directly about the Heriot-Watt Foundation English course and said that it had helped with notes, referencing and citation:

> *Erm it's a good way to get me to keep forward because I don't need to know how to write the notes or reference and I have known how to write the style how to write the dissertation and er erm it's always helps me with the language* (CS).

Several participants said that the English course had also helped:

> *Because I'm not nervous to listen and I can also ask some questions to others, to other people* (CS),

saying of the structure of dissertations on the Master's course, in China, and in the project they had done on their EAP course that

> *Yeh It's all the same* (CS).

Although another participant said that the structure of the dissertation in China and on the English course was different:

in Chinese write the dissertation the first er in Foundation English the first include aim but in China we need er first paragraph we need make some process the structure is different (CS).

Another participant said the English course had helped them because

before you do a Master's you have a good English to do I mean you should have a good quality of English ... [and that it was] ... very useful knowing knowing the plagiarism is very important For our work our future work (CS).

Here again the comments support the usefulness of the EAP courses for these participants, their experiences on EAP courses helping them in their subsequent courses.

4.1.3. The difficulty of 'Plagiarism'

Of the four participants who spoke of the difficulty of plagiarism, three of them had not done EAP courses before, one noting that in China

we don't care much about the copyright so we can just copy others, so it's (unclear) I like this (laughs) [Interviewer Was it easy?] Yeh I think much easier than here (CS),

or another that

in English you must read it understanding and writing use your language that is difference and er however (CS),

and another participant on whether it was difficult to cite others' work for all students or just students from China said

I think students from China (AS).

However, one participant who had done the EAP course at Heriot-Watt spoke at length about having to go to the discipline committee with regard to plagiarism:

I meet ... a problem of the cultural style because in China if you copy some words from the other person We just er write the name of the book and the reference But here I think the people they pay more attention to the copyright more than more than China ... [Interviewer - Uh huh Didn't you do this last year on the English course?] ... Yeh I think in that I do it not enough because I met some problem when I do the course So

> *when I do the dissertation I will pay more attention to the copyright This is very important to Chinese everyone from China have this ... because our class have seven Chinese but er four of us four of us have the problem in the coursework the tutor said we have copied too much from the web or from the book and the committee the discipline committee ... They get the result we have we have failed in the whole module* (CS).

In a later interview the same participant said

> *I have known before I can't copy and plagiarism just er erm the way the method I use in this dissertation sometimes don't equal sometime I just got the idea from other people but I use my own words* (CS),

and at the end of the interview commented that

> *my confusion about how to do the reference* (CS).

On the whole, these comments indicate that dealing with plagiarism was found more challenging by the participants who had not done any EAP preparation courses before their studies. The one anomaly is the participant who had done an EAP course and still found it very hard to avoid plagiarism, still being unsure, even at the end of their Master's course, as to how to avoid plagiarism.

When the eighteen continuing participants were asked whether they found using quotes and references difficult in both interviews two and three, the picture that emerges is a complex one with some students changing in their perceptions of difficulty. By the third interview, six of the eighteen participants said they found it difficult (and of these, three had done EAP courses) and twelve said they did not find it difficult (three of whom had done EAP courses).

4.1.4. Knowledge of the dissertation at the outset

Twenty one participants were asked 'What do you know about the dissertation at Heriot-Watt?' Out of seventeen participants who said they knew something about the dissertation, eight who had studied EAP courses or undergraduate courses expressed some knowledge of the dissertation. Of the four who said they knew very little or nothing, two had previously studied EAP courses.

The results here are thus somewhat inconclusive: the majority of those who had studied EAP courses had a knowledge of the dissertation at the outset, but then again, so did a number of participants who had not.

4.1.5. Difficulties

When asked what their most significant difficulty was, six participants said language (three of whom had done an EAP course). Another eleven participants mentioned difficulties that were mainly content related (three of these had done an EAP course) and one participant said that they had not had any significant difficulties.

Here again the results are inconclusive. Language was considered the major difficulty by both participants who had done EAP courses and by participants who had not. It could of course be argued that the EAP course had made participants more aware of the necessity for language and of the challenges they would need to face in this area, and also that despite having followed an EAP course they still needed to work on their language abilities.

4.2. Section B: Challenges for EAP

4.2.1. Differences in dissertations

Some participants commented upon differences in dissertations; these comments related to a number of levels. Two participants noted the difference between dissertations in their departments, one saying of the dissertation they were doing that

> *the requirement about this dissertation I think is a bit higher than some others* (AS),

but another that

> *I think I didn't have to spend everyday on it* ....[Interviewer – Have you told the students in the other groups this?] (laughs) *they envy me because they are just struggling now and I have finished* [Interviewer - (laughs)](AS).

Similarly, in another department one participant said they had

> *finish my project in two weeks and dissertation in two weeks* (CS),

whereas another noted that

> *it's a lot of work.... I made much effort on this project 8 hours I need 8 hours per day but I mean the real challenge is to carry out the dissertation* (CS).

Three other participants commented on these kinds of differences.

On a cross-departmental level, one participant commented that

> *the dissertation for MSc students of Actuarial* [Science] *is not so highly requirement as in some other subjects such as Logistics* (AS)

Two participants also mentioned inequities across different universities, one saying that, in terms of supervision, they knew someone who had done an MSc elsewhere in the UK and that the course

> *was not well arranged ... because there were around 200 students far far too many firstly, secondly er they they did find very difficult to contact or getting some help from their tutors Because they were very busy and even if you make a appointment or something they don't have enough time to give* (AS),

or that another that

> *in er British education but also the universities are different because I think Heriot-Watt in the science is very good but er you know [name of other UK] university maybe I many friends in that university studying science and business management ...I think that education is easy Yes no stress* (CS).

These results are included here to show the range of dissertations that EAP students are going on to do. This raises a challenge for EAP in preparing students for their courses and suggests the need to allow for tailoring of EAP courses to specific subject needs where possible.

4.2.2. Comments about Chinese students

A number of participants saw Chinese students as being homogenous and having similar difficulties (three from CS and four from AS) one saying that

> *I have a very nice mind to carry out the dissertation but I can't write it write down it's main problem for most Chinese students* (CS).

Two participants (both from CS) commented on how they saw Mainland Chinese students as being separate from Taiwanese and Hong Kong students, one saying that

I can tell you we are different with Hong Kong students and Taiwanese because we, we have our own erm how to say traditional methods to write erm papers (CS).

However, two participants commented on the differences in students coming from China, of how students with work experience would approach the dissertation with more aim and diligence than those without (AS) and another of how those who have done their degree in the UK have less of an aim and are less hardworking than those who have done their UG degree in China

because I've talked to some student who have been here since their high school age and they're not so clear about their future, that's the main difference I believe (AS).

These results are included to highlight the different changing nature of the students coming to study in the UK and the different possible backgrounds of the students from Mainland China. This shows a system in flux and this is mirrored by the comments above and by much of the literature on Chinese learners (Clark & Gieve, 2004; Jin & Cortazzi, 2006) and is one of the challenges facing EAP tutors as well as departments.

4.3. Section C: The need for EAP

4.3.1. Academic practice in the UK and China

Some participants mentioned that Britain was more relaxed than China, that with regard to students doing set tutorial work, in China

it's essential I think here it's er you can do it or you can not do it, just depends on you (AS).

Similarly, that the supervision in China would be far more directive:

I'd like to say the difference between Chinese supervisors and British supervisors Coz in Chinese your supervisor will tell you what you should do next ... very detailed tell you how to do that ... but here erm the supervisor's like a guide ... actually in this situation I think we can learn more than than the case in China (AS).

However, another participant said that

I think in China the students I mean the teacher, the supervisor will tell the students what they should do and how to do ... I think now I'm studying in UK so that's enough, it's my problem [Interviewer – OK, are you happy with it?] (pause) *Not so happy, I think they should more details about the projects, the different projects* (AS).

Yet, another participant's experience was of a very non-directive supervisor in China, saying that

my supervisor in China I think is not very good, I think he's not very good er everything is all on me I I do everything (CS).

Also, two participants experience was that there was more of a structure to the dissertation here,

I know it's different from very different with what I do in the University in China Er I think it's more ... systematic than in China (CS),

or that

in China we don't have the presentation (CS).

In terms of supervision, one participant noted how tutors were always available in China, but not here:

we can communicate with them in maybe holiday or maybe we can't in UK I find just our professor told us which day should we meet we should come or not, it's very difficult to make appointment maybe professor here is very busy (AS).

The fact that the content of the dissertation is different in the UK, that in the UK there's a big literature review but not in China, was also commented on:

in China we just write er er simple piece of paper called how do you understand you're your project title ... so it's quite easy but here with the literature review you have to read a lot of things^3 (CS).

Or that the process was different:

Er, Ah I should I should point, in China we always write code first, write project first and then give the dissertation but here I think it's some kind of upside down you write dissertation first and then write code erm I a little confusion I don't know how to do (CS).

Or that the approach to collaborative work was different:

in China ... we do our dissertations ourselves not work with other people ... But in this dissertation I should work with another partner, the smallest group is er two people (AS).

Interestingly, one participant's experience had been that studying the Heriot-Watt EAP course had been very different to China, but that the Master's had been the same

during the studying English ... the skills for lectures is very good not like in China ... the class is very bored very boring But here the class er is vivid is very active I can er learn more and very effective to improve my English in class it's big big it's difference between education system in China and in Britain here I have learned lots of things [Interviewer – and on the Master's?] *Er Master's is the same Master's the same situation as in within China education system lecturers just teach you and then maybe she maybe she don't know you after graduation So I mean the relationship between the lecturer and student is not very close here same same as in China* (CS).

These results are included to illustrate the need for EAP in terms of the different experiences students coming to the UK from mainland China have had. Many students have had different experiences in China from what they have experienced in the UK although interestingly one participant found their experience on the Master's course similar to their previous course in China but that their EAP course had been very different. From what these participants said it is suggested there is a need to prepare students in the best way possible which arguably means preparing them for what they will encounter on their Master's courses.

4.3.2. Support within the subject departments

Participants were not asked directly about whether a Research Methods course run in their department was useful but nonetheless two commented on this course, one positively:

it's very useful...lots of knowledges about how to carry out the dissertation (CS).

Another participant, however, thought it was only useful to an extent, saying that *it's quite helpful but ... different people have different requirements any lecturers can't fulfil everybody's requirements* (CS).

These comments are included by way of an addendum to illustrate the difficulties that the departments also have in preparing students for their dissertations, and to argue that the challenges facing EAP are similar to those faced by departments as well.

5. Conclusion

The data and results presented here show an initial support for EAP. They show that generally speaking, the interviewed participants who had done EAP courses looked upon them favourably. This is supported by comments from the participants relating to courses in English for General Purposes and exam preparation courses stating that these courses were not much use (See above Section A Unsolicited references to English Courses). In terms of knowledge about plagiarism the participants who had done EAP courses or study in the UK generally knew more about this although there were exceptions. The challenges for EAP tutors in the face of the wide range of dissertations and the wide ranging nature of students coming to EAP courses is to remain up to date and to cater for many different students (Hyland, 2002). That there is, nevertheless, a need for EAP is championed by these two factors above and also by comments relating to the differing situations in academia (Ballard & Clanchy, 1991; Gay Fitzgerald, 2003) that continue to exist elsewhere and in the way in which departmental provision is perceived. Yet, the comments from the participants interviewed in this study are still few in number and more data needs to be gathered. It is hoped that the next stage of the study this author is undertaking this year will gather data from a similar number of participants and that this can add to the body of data that exists already. It is also suggested that to further establish the success of EAP courses more links with departments are made to better cater for students going on to courses and more suggestions to the needs of prospective students can be made by these departments. As an indication of the need for further research and collection of data, one participant recently interviewed as part of the data collection for the second year said the following:

since I've been here I've never heard anybody said Oh my God my language course so useful ... I never heard that ... I never heard that, I only heard is like Oh my god my language course is so expensive and it's so useless and it's so tiring, that's what I heard (CS).

Notes

[1] Students follow part or all of the course depending upon their level of entry and the course they are progressing on to.

[2] Students interviewed were in the Department of Computer Science (CS) and the Department of Actuarial Science (AS)

[3] It is possible here that the participant is comparing a past experience of an undergraduate dissertation, or of a dissertation in a subject that did not require a literature review, i.e. that the student is not comparing like with like.

References

Allison, D. (2004). Creativity, students' academic writing, and EAP: Exploring comments on writing in an English language degree programme. *Journal of English for Academic Purposes, 3*, 191-210.

Ballard, B. & Clanchy, J. (1991). *Teaching students from overseas: A Brief guide for lecturers and supervisors.* Melbourne: Longman Cheshire.

Bannerjee, J. & Wall, D. (2006). Assessing and reporting performances on Pre-Sessional EAP course: Developing a final assessment checklist and investigating its validity. *Journal of English for Academic Purposes, 5,* 50-69.

Bitchener, J. & Basturkman, H. (2006). Perceptions of the difficulties of postgraduate L2 thesis students writing the discussion section. *Journal of English for Academic Purposes, 5,* 4-18

Bochner, S. (1980). Unobtrusive methods in cross-cultural experimentation. In H. C. Triandis & J. W. Berry (Eds.), *Handbook of cross-cultural psychology. Volume 2. Methodology.* Boston: Allyn and Bacon.

Clark, M. K. & Ishida, S. (2005). Vocabulary knowledge differences between placed and promoted EAP students. *Journal of English for Academic Purposes, 4, 225-238*

Clark, R. & Gieve, S. (2004). *On the discursive construction of 'the Chinese learner'.* Paper presented at 'Responding to the needs of the Chinese learner in higher education' conference, University of Portsmouth

Cortazzi, M. & Jin, L. (2004). *Changing practices in Chinese cultures of learning.* Paper presented at 'Responding to the needs of the Chinese learner in higher education' conference, University of Portsmouth

Cohen, L. & Manion, L. (1994). *Research methods in education* (4th ed.). London: Routledge

Crowne, D. P. & Marlowe, D. (1964). *The approval motive.* New York: Wiley.

Gay Fitzgerald, H. (2003). *How different are we? Spoken discourse in intercultural communication: The significance of the situational context.* Clevedon: Multilingual Matters Ltd.

Gubrium, J. F. & Holstein, J. A. (2000). Analysing interpretive practice. In N. K Denzin & Y. S. Lincoln (Eds.), *Handbook of qualitative research* (2nd ed.) (pp. 487-508). Thousand Oaks, CA: Sage.

Harwood, N, (2005). What do we want EAP teaching materials for? *Journal of English for Academic Purposes, 4,* 149-162.

Hycner, R. H (1999). Some guidelines for the phenomenological analysis of interview data. In A. Bryman & R. G. Burgess (Eds.) *Qualitative research: Volume 3.* Thousand Oaks, CA: Sage.

Hyland, K. & Hamp-Lyons, L. (2002). EAP: Issues and directions. *Journal of English for Academic Purposes, 1,* 1-12.

Hyland, K. (2002). Specificity revisited: How far should we go? *Journal of English for Specific Purposes, 21,* 385-396.

Jin, L. & Cortazzi, M. (2006). Changing practices in Chinese cultures of learning. *Language, Culture & Curriculum, 19,* 5-20.

Kirkpatrick, A. (2004). Some thoughts on the Chinese learner and the teaching of writing. *The East Asian Learner, 1*(1).

Moore, T. & Morton, J. (2005). Dimensions of difference: a comparison of university writing and IELTS writing. *Journal of English for Academic Purposes, 4,* 43-66.

Orne, M. T. (1962). On the social psychology of the psychological experiment: with particular reference to demand characteristics and their implications. *American Psychologist, 17,* 776-783.

Orne, M. T. (1970). Hypnosis, motivation, and the ecological validity of the psychological experiment. In W. J. Arnold & M. M. Page (Eds.), *Nebraska symposium on motivation* (pp. 187-285). Lincoln: University of Nebraska Press.

Powney, J. & Watts, M. (1987). *Interviewing in educational research.* London: Routledge and Kegan Paul.

Silverman, D. (2000). Doing *qualitative research: A practical handbook.* Thousand Oaks, CA: Sage Publications.

Appendix A

Interview questions for the students

1. Your concept of a dissertation

Have you written a dissertation before? How long was it? What was your experience of doing it?
What have you read about the dissertation at Heriot Watt?

What do you know about the dissertation at Heriot Watt?
What are the aims of the dissertation for you? For the department?
Why are you doing the dissertation?
I'm interviewing students in Computing / Actuarial Science, you are in Computing / Actuarial Science, do you think the dissertations are different in the other department? How / why
What are the benefits of doing the dissertation? Why is it useful? What are the academic, professional and personal benefits?

2. The structure of a dissertation

What do you think the sequence of the dissertation is? What comes first? Next? What should the dissertation include?

3. Your perception of a good dissertation

What do you think makes a good dissertation?
What about a bad dissertation?
How would you judge this?
What do you think you will need to do to write a good dissertation?
Some people say writing a dissertation is like a journey, what was your journey like?

4. The difficulties of writing a dissertation

What do you think the difficulties of writing a dissertation are?
What difficulties are you finding?
What advice would you give to other students next year for writing a dissertation?
Can you describe to me how you prepare and write your dissertation?

5. The guidance received for writing the dissertation

What guidance have you been given for the dissertation so far? Is this enough? Are you happy with it? What about the tutorials? Are / were they useful? How / Why / why not?
What qualities do you think a good supervisor has?

6. The interview

Do you think I have missed anything important about doing a dissertation?
Would you like to know what others think about something? What?
Did you feel relaxed or nervous during the interview?
Was this time OK for you? What about this place?
Would you like to ask me any questions about my Master's dissertation?

Measuring gains in oral performance on Pre-Sessional courses

John Morley, The University of Manchester

Abstract

One important aim of Pre-Sessional courses is the development of students' oral proficiency, for academic purposes and also for general use. Measuring gains in oral proficiency over a relatively short period presents a number of challenges. For one thing, impressionistic assessments based on band descriptors are not sufficiently reliable or refined to measure modest gains in this area. Furthermore, the quality of a speaker's production may vary at different times depending on a number of factors. This paper examines a range of more objective measurements of oral proficiency. Specifically, it discusses a number of techniques for obtaining fairly precise quantitative measures of spoken fluency, complexity and accuracy. Some of the methods described may also be used to gauge degrees of change in the quality of student writing.

1. Introduction

One of the aims of university Pre-Sessional courses is the development of students' oral performance for both academic and general purposes. Improved oral performance may sometimes be seen as secondary to the more important aim of developing students' academic literacy skills, but we need to remember that most non-native speakers join Pre-Sessional courses because they have not attained a sufficient level of language competence – not necessarily because they lack certain academic skills, though this is usually also the case. So for the students, for their sponsors and for their lecturers, the development of oral competence, along with the development of other areas of linguistic competence, is of importance, and showing evidence of gains in students' oral proficiency would be one way of demonstrating the usefulness of university Pre-Sessional courses.

Using impressionistic ratings of students' performances on speaking tests would seem to be one way of measuring gains in oral proficiency. However, such assessments are not sufficiently reliable or refined to measure modest gains in this area over a very short period of time, and there are a number of reasons for this. For one thing, with such assessments the learner's performance needs to be interpreted by a rater, and different raters do not always agree on the same score. According to Brown (1995, p. 13), even where standardisation training has taken place, raters have different perceptions 'about what is acceptable' (see also Langley, 2002[1]). Added to the difficulty of standardising interpretations is the fact that, in many formalised assessments (e.g. IELTS), raters attempt to measure different aspects of language concurrently in real time during fairly short interviews, which is very difficult. In fact, at any particular time, the rater can only focus on one aspect of oral performance, and as a range of performance elements are normally measured, in a brief interview each of these will only be measured for a short period of time. This is a significant weakness if we accept that the quality of different elements of oral production may vary considerably over the course of a short interview. If the oral assessments involve interviews with trained interviewers, a further challenge to reliability arises. In an investigation into the IELTS speaking test, Brown found that the interviewer a student encounters can 'significantly affect their chances of achieving a desired score' (2005, p. 243). Variable features of interviewer behaviour may include the type of interactional strategies employed, the relationship they established with the candidates and their questioning technique and speech style. The other thing that we need to bear in mind is the fact that the band descriptors used in such assessment procedures are fairly blunt instruments. For example, the IELTS band descriptors range from 1 (absolute beginner) to 9 (educated native speaker standard), but any given band may actually represent a fairly a wide range of competency levels for each element of oral performance that is being assessed.

The purpose of this paper, therefore, is to examine a range of alternative, more accurate and objective measurements of oral proficiency. Specifically, it will discuss a number of techniques for obtaining fairly precise quantitative measures of oral performance over relatively short periods of time, such as at the beginning and end of a 10 or 12 week Pre-Sessional course. Some of the methods described might also be applied to gauge degrees of change in the quality of student writing over similar periods of time.

2. What can be measured?

There is a consensus in the literature that three general dimensions of oral performance, which are fluency, accuracy and complexity, and which broadly reflect learner goals, can be measured fairly precisely and reliably, and provide useful quantitative indices for comparative purposes (Skehan, 1998). Definitions of each of these dimensions have been provided by Skehan (1996). Fluency is understood in a narrow sense in which highly-rated students are those whose speech approaches native-like rapidity and is unimpeded by silent pauses, hesitations, filled pauses, corrections, repetitions and false starts. Accuracy refers to 'how well the target language is produced in relation to the rule system

73

of the target language' (Skehan, 1996, p. 23). Complexity can relate to various aspects of language production[2]. However, in its narrow sense it refers to the degree to which the speaker is able to or is prepared to use a wide range of lexis and grammatical structures, or in Skehan's words (1996, p. 22) 'the elaboration or ambition of the language that is produced'. Together, these dimensions encompass most of the linguistic elements of oral performance, particularly if phonological quality is also included under this definition of accuracy.

In more fluent production, meaning and communication tend to be prioritised, and in more accurate and complex language production attention to form is prioritised. Although they have been theorised as having independent functioning, they also enter into competition with one another, with good performance in one detracting from the performance in another (Skehan, 1998). The generally accepted explanation of this is that we have limited attentional capacity (Baddeley, 1986), and we simply do not have the cognitive resources to attend to many things simultaneously. In real time language production, most non-native speakers are unable to give sufficient attention to both meaning and content, which is reflected in fluent production, and at the same time give sufficient attention to lexical retrieval, syntactic building procedures, and phonological encoding (Levelt, 1988), which manifests as accuracy and complexity. However, with increasing practice, these latter processes become increasingly automatised, and language can thus be stored and retrieved as prefabricated chunks or patterns, thus resulting in more fluent production. Because the speaker does not have to create new constructions with reference to a rule based system, they are able to devote more of their attentional resources to content and meaning. There also seems to be a trade-off between increased complexity and accuracy, with more complex production demanding greater attentional resource but also tending to produce a greater number of errors. However, this latter phenomenon may be a result of the speaker being more prepared to take risks with unfamiliar structures and/or lexical items rather than just because of limitations of attentional capacity.

Quantitative measures of fluency, accuracy and complexity have been utilised in studies which have investigated the effectiveness of pedagogic tasks and how different performance conditions affect oral output. This body of research is now quite considerable and examples of areas of investigations have included: the effects of different conditions operating during pre-task planning on the variables of fluency, accuracy, and complexity (Foster & Skehan, 1996); the impact of task repetition on fluency, accuracy, and complexity (Bygate, 2001); the effects of different task characteristics on fluency, accuracy, and complexity (Skehan, 2001); and the influence of surprise information and task time on performance on these performance variables (Skehan & Foster, 2005). Typical research design in these investigations has been to compare the output of different groups of students (n = 15 - 30 per group) who perform tasks under differing conditions. Various measures for fluency, accuracy and complexity are then analysed using descriptive and comparative statistics. The measures used in these studies do seem to be able to detect fairly modest changes in performance.

However, if our aim is to measure changes in oral performance over time, for example at the beginning and end of a Pre-Sessional EAP course, a different design is necessary. For one thing, we would want to compare changes in oral performance within the same group, obtaining a 'snapshot' of students' performance at the beginning of the course (time 1) and comparing this with a snapshot of language at the end of the course (time 2). This type of design has been used fairly extensively in studies which have investigated the impact of a period of study abroad on second language oral production. The following studies, for example, all concerned with trying to measure the effect of a short period abroad on learner fluency, have used this model (Freed, 1995; Freed, Segalowitz & Dewey, 2004; Segalowitz & Freed, 2004; Towell, Hawkins & Bazergui, 1996). This latter study compared the fluency gains of a group of students on a seven week French immersion course with that of a group of students who studied French in Paris for 12 weeks, and found that, though of shorter duration, the intensive nature of the immersion programme resulted in greater gains in fluency.

In many studies which measure changes in aspects of oral proficiency, the language under study is monologic in character. Oral narrative tasks, for example, have been used by many researchers (e.g. Bygate, 2001; Foster & Skehan, 1996, 1999; Kawauchi, 2005; Skehan & Foster, 1997; Towell, Hawkins & Bazergui, 1996; Yuan and Ellis, 2003). Such tasks allow us to obtain measurements of performance that are not affected by interactional variables such as the degree of backchanneling, the quantity and type of paralinguistic feedback, the unpredictable dynamics of the interaction. However, this is not always the case, and Foster and Skehan's work includes a number of studies in which performance on interactive tasks is measured (e.g. Skehan, 2001; Skehan & Foster, 1999). Other criteria for task selection are that they are reasonably linguistically demanding, and that they have the potential to elicit around five minutes of language output. Neutrality of content is another important attribute. In a study to do with oral performance gain on a 12 week Pre-Sessional course, it would be tempting to use an authentic task, for example, an academic presentation relating to the student's prospective subject. This would be motivating and interesting for the student, and it could be argued that we are

75

creating an authentic context for language measurement. However, the problem is that with such a task it would be impossible to control for content difficulty and/or content familiarity and so the results would be unreliable. Finally, because differing task conditions and task characteristics can affect oral performance, and will push learners to perform in certain ways, prioritising one or another aspect of language (Skehan, 2001), the linguistic output that we wish to study has to be obtained under identical conditions using very similar, but not the same, tasks at time 1 and time 2. Any change in performance detected using identical tasks could be attributed to a task repetition effect (Bygate, 2001).

3. Measurements of fluency

Temporal variables of speech have been used to measure two broad dimensions of fluency. These are aspects associated with rate of production and aspects associated with flow and smoothness. Productivity can be measured in terms of rate of production over a given time. Thus production rate can be computed by the number of words produced per minute (Freed, Segalowitz & Dewey, 2004) or the number of syllables produced per minute (Ellis & Yuan, 2005; Towell, Hawkins & Bazergui, 1996). Number of syllables per minute avoids the problem of varying word length affecting the measurements. Flow and smoothness relate primarily to such phenomena as the extent of silent and filled pausing during production. Simple measures include: the total number of pauses greater than one second per five minutes of performance (Skehan, 2001). More sophisticated, however, is the mean length of pause free runs in syllables, commonly known as mean length run (MLR), between pauses of a certain length. This measure has been used extensively in the literature (Freed, 1995; Freed, Segalowitz & Dewey, 2004; Möehle, 1984; Riggenbach, 1991; Towell, Hawkins & Bazergui, 1996). Another variable of fluency, which is associated with flow and smoothness, is what might be termed the breakdown dimension. This has been measured in terms of the number of repetitions, reformulations/repairs, false starts, and replacements per five minutes of speech (Skehan & Foster, 1999) or per number of words produced (Ellis & Yuan, 2005). As a variation, Freed, Segalowitz & Dewey (2004) measured the mean number of words before repetition or reformulation/repair occurred.

In an attempt to gain more insight into these types of measurements studies have been carried out in which samples of speech produced by non-native speakers of English were judged by experienced experts for fluency and were then analysed in terms of different variables, such as speech production rate, and length of fluent speech run. One of the first applied linguists to investigate which measures were able to clearly distinguish the speech of highly fluent non-native speakers from non-fluent non-native speakers was Heidi Riggenbach (1990). Riggenbach carried out a detailed analysis of the speech of six non-native speakers who represented examples of highly fluent and non-fluent speakers. These two subgroups were identified by a panel of twelve ESL instructors using a seven point open-ended scale. She concluded the two most important components of non-native speaker fluency might include: i) hesitation phenomena - frequency, placement and degree of chunking, and type of filled and unfilled pauses; and ii) rate of speech. A larger scale study by Ejzenburg (1992 in Freed, 1995) analysed the perceived non-native fluency of 50 Brazilian students of English. Examining the profiles of three high and three low frequency speakers, Ejzenburg was able to show that high-fluency speakers tend to speak both more and faster than fluent speakers with speech rate standing out as the most distinguishing variable between the two groups. Ejzenburg also found that the speech of high-fluency subjects contained longer 'talk units' and longer 'fluent units' with 'fluent unit lengths' proving to be the more sensitive of the two factors in predicting levels of subject fluency (1992, p. 195).

Tonkyn (2001) analysed the speech of eight non-native speakers of English whose fluency levels were assessed by four raters trained to assess learners using the Cambridge International English Language Testing System (IELTS) bands. For this exercise, he created an analytical rating scale for fluency of nine bands derived from the composite IELTS scale. The eight students were assessed at Band 6 by at least three of the four raters, with the fourth rating differing by no more than half a band or one band. The speech of these students was compared with the speech of one student who had unanimously been rated at Band 4 by the same raters. A range of measures was used to analyse the speech samples including: productivity (e.g. number of words per unit of speech), amount of pausing (e.g. mean length run), placement of pauses, rate of speech (e.g. syllables per second), vocal fluency (e.g. frequency of self-corrections and repetitions). Following close comparison of the samples, Tonkyn concludes that 'the features of productivity, length of fluent run, speaking rate and number of extraneous words might be the best features on which to focus' (Tonkyn, 2001, p. 9). At the same time, he does point out that these features may only be significant when contrasting upper intermediate speech samples with lower intermediate samples, and of course to draw firm conclusions from such a small sample would be careless.

Taken together, however, these evaluative studies suggest that both speaking rate and mean length of fluent run appear to be useful quantitative objective measures of a speaker's fluency. With the latter measure there is some debate about the cut-off point for measuring pauses between fluent runs of speech.

Although a number of researchers have used cut-off points of less than 0.4 seconds (e.g. Goldman-Eisler, 1968; Raupach, 1987; Towell, 1996), Riggenbach (1991) suggested that pauses shorter than 0.4 seconds are within the range of normal or fluent speech and do not reflect dysfluency. Riggenbach's suggestion is supported by Freed (1995) who explains that when native speakers were asked to listen to recorded extracts of non-native speakers and to mark disfluent pauses on transcripts, the pauses they marked tended to be .4 seconds or longer. Another decision that needs to be made is whether to count filled or unfilled pauses, or both (Freed, 2004; Towell, Hawkins & Bazergui, 1996). Filled pauses are hesitations filled with items such as *uhhh* or *errrr*. For accurate measurements of this kind, some kind of speech analysis tool is required. *Speech Analyser* (SIL, 1996) developed by the Summer Institute of Linguistics can be downloaded for free, but other analysis software is also available.

4. Measurements of complexity

We have already seen how complexity, in the grammatical/lexical sense, takes into account both sophistication and range of structures or lexical items produced. Measures of grammatical complexity fall into two main groups. The first of these consists of measures that analyse the units of language in terms of each other. Many of these are concerned with the extent to which subordination is used in relation to some independent structural unit. A number of recent studies, for example, have calculated the mean number of clauses per 'T-unit'[3] in monologic speech performances as a measure of syntactic complexity. Yuan & Ellis (2003, 2005) and Kawauchi (2005) found that this variable is quite sensitive to differing conditions affecting speech performance. Foster, Tonkyn Wigglesworth (2000) point out that the number of clauses per 'T-unit' works less well for interactive speech as this typically contains large numbers of sub-clausal units. They propose that a more useful unit of analysis is the Analysis of Speech Unit[4] or 'AS unit'. Clause-based measures of complexity have been used with written texts. In a major meta-analysis of measures used to measure learners' development in writing, Wolfe-Quintero, Inagaki & Kim (1998) found that the number of clauses per 'T-unit' (C/T) and the number of dependent clauses per clause (CD/C) were the best measures. In evaluating the measures, the researchers used two criteria: the first of these was reliable and consistent progression of the measure across externally-determined proficiency levels; the second was a statistically significant and highly correlated relationship between the measure and either programme or school levels.

One of the issues that arises with clause-based studies of this kind is how clause units are defined since adverbial, nominal, and adjectival clauses can all be reduced to participle phrases or prepositional phrases. Reductions of clauses to phrases will certainly affect the clause count, and this could result in a text with a high number of reduced forms being analysed as less sophisticated. However, these reduced forms may be a characteristic of the speech of more advanced speakers. Indeed, Hunt (1965) proposed that, in writing, grammatical complexity in written language develops from coordination to subordination to reduced phrases. And Sharma (1980) has suggested that whilst use of relative clauses is an indication of sophisticated production, at more advances levels they may decrease in favour of adjectives and prepositional phrases. This has led some researchers to count non-finite verb phrases which do not have subjects as clauses (Wolfe-Quintero, Inagaki & Kim, 1998, p. 72). A simpler version of the 'T-unit' measure, which largely avoids the need to define and count clauses, is the number of words per 'T-unit'. Bygate (2001) used this in an interesting study which found that this complexity measure was sensitive to task repetition after a period of 10 weeks. In the same study, perhaps less surprisingly, this measure was also shown to be sensitive to different task type.

The second set of complexity measures are concerned with specific grammatical features. One of the specific complexity variables which Yuan & Ellis (2003) set out to measure in their recent study of language produced under different operating conditions was syntactic variety. They did this by counting the total number of verb forms used in each task for each individual. Grammatical verb forms which were used for the analysis were tense (e.g. simple past, past continuous), modality (e.g. should, have to), and voice (e.g. passive voice in the past). However, whilst the different operating conditions did noticeably affect this variable, none of the differences were found to be significant. Another interesting specific measure is the total number of verb arguments (subjects, direct objects, indirect objects, adjectival complements, prepositional phrases) divided by the total number of verbs (Bygate, 1999). A higher proportion of arguments is indicative of a more sophisticated nominal style of speech. A related measure that could be useful for measuring change in grammatical sophistication over time has to do with the complexity of the noun phrase. We know that nominal complexity[5] in L2 writing is significantly related to leaner age and level of study (Cooper, 1976) and it may be that a similar pattern can be found with learner speech. Cooper measured the number of complex nominals per 'T-unit', but a variation of this could be the average number of words per grammatical subject. It is clear, however, that more research needs to be done on just how the measures concerned with aspects of nominalisation in speech relate to the more general measures described earlier. A high score on some of these measures could correlate with a lower score on one of the clause/unit measures described earlier since greater normalisation may result, for example, in fewer clause units per 'T-unit'.

As well as grammatical complexity, we might also wish to consider lexical complexity as an aspect of oral production. A high level of lexical complexity means that speech is characterised by a wide range of basic and sophisticated words. Measures of lexical complexity are not concerned with the number of words but with how varied the words or word types are, and this is generally measured by calculating type-token ratio - the closer the type-token ratio is to one, the greater the lexical richness (Ellis & Barkhuizem, 2005). The type-token ratio is calculated in the following way: if a text is 1000 words long, it is said to have 1000 tokens. However, many of these words will be repeated and there may only be 400 different words in the text. In this case, the ratio between types and tokens (TTR) would be 40%. One problem with this is that type token ratio is affected by different lengths of text, with shorter texts producing higher ratios. When comparing texts, therefore, it is important to ensure that they are all of a similar length. A number of different software tools for measuring TTR are available. One of the best is *Wordsmith 4* (Scott, 2004). This programme uses a measure which gets round the problem of texts of different lengths: the Standardised Type Token Ratio[6] (STTR), which is computerised for every set number of words.

However, with one or two exceptions (e.g. Yuan & Ellis, 2003), this does not seem to be a very sensitive measure for speech productions. Perhaps one reason for this is that speech productions are typically characterised by narrow lexical range with most words being frequently used items. In fact, a fairly narrow range of words will allow us to do and say most things, and this means that, when producing spoken language in real time, the differences in lexical range between less proficient students and more advanced students may not be very marked. The only way around this would be to attempt to elicit productions which could demonstrate knowledge or lack of knowledge of the lexis associated with particular specialised domains. However, the ability to perform well on such a task would be contingent on the degree to which the learners were familiar with the domain and it would be dangerous to extrapolate from this to some general score for lexical range. Another problem with this measure is that whilst it gives an indication of lexical range, it does not account for lexical precision nor can it take account of the use of lexical phrases which are probably typical of the speech of more advanced speakers. It may be for this reason that measurements of lexical complexity are not commonly used in studies of oral performance; nevertheless, a number of studies (see Wolfe-Quintero, Inagaki & Kim, 1998, pp. 104-115) have found this and other lexical ratio measures to be a useful indicator to measure the complexity of learners' writing.

5. Measurements of accuracy

Earlier, accuracy was defined as 'how well the target language is produced in relation to the rule system of the target language' (Skehan, 1996, p. 23). In other words, it is the extent to which a person avoids making errors while using language to communicate either in speech or in writing. Foster and Skehan and Foster (1999, p. 229) suggest that generalised measures of accuracy such as the percentage of error free clauses and errors per 100 words, are 'more sensitive to detecting differences between experimental conditions'. The first of these was used by Ellis & Yuan (2003, 2005) to measure the effects of different kinds of task planning on spoken performance and it showed a large effect size. Using a slightly different measure, Bygate (2001) found that the number of errors per 'T-unit' somewhat insensitive to different effects (task repetition and task-type) since one or two 'exploratory but error-strewn utterances can compromise an otherwise error free performance' (p.43), and he proposes that it might be more useful to calculate the number of error free 'T- units' in order to assess performance. These clause-based measures of accuracy do seem to be effective in measuring short-term changes in writing. In their meta-analysis of developmental measures in writing Wolfe-Quintero, Inagaki & Kim (1998) analysed over 27 accuracy ratios used in 81 different studies. They conclude that the accuracy measures that were significantly related to short term change across a range of levels and within groups of learners were error free 'T-units' per 'T-unit' and errors per 'T-unit'.

One of the issues that arises with this type of measure, indeed with nearly all measures of accuracy, is that there may not be a linear relationship between accuracy and other dimensions of proficiency, with some advanced students taking more risks and/or using more sophisticated language and thus making more errors due to greater complexity. In fact, Larsen-Freeman (1983) found that, in writing, learners peaked in their error free 'T-unit' ratio at intermediate level writing and then decreased at more advanced levels. In contrast, Henry (1995) found that scores on the error-free T-unit ratio for timed essays increased from the first to second semesters of university Russian study, but decreased at the fourth semester, but then increased again at the sixth semester. It is very likely that such trade-off effects occur in speaking as well. Any study attempting to assess gains in oral performance, therefore, should look for evidence of possible trade-off effects between fluency, complexity and accuracy. Other problems with these generalised measures concern determining exactly what constitutes an error and how self-corrected clauses or errors are counted.

Alongside the more generalised measures of accuracy exist a number of possible measures that focus on specific aspects for language production. One of these is the percentage of target-like verbal morphology (Wigglesworth, 1997; Yuan & Ellis, 2003). This is a measure of the correct number of finite verb phrases divided by the total number of verb phrases multiplied by 100. Another specific measure that seems to have been fairly widely used is the percentage of correct past tense markers. (Kawauchi, 2005), for example, showed that with advanced speakers, the percentage of correct past tense forms was higher in planned narratives than in unplanned narratives. This effect was particularly significant with the irregular forms. The validity of such measures depends on the extent to which a learner's ability to use this specific measure correlates with their overall grammatical competence. This assumption may be questionable, and is unlikely to be the same for students from different L1 backgrounds. Ellis & Barkhuizem (2005) argue that such measures are best used alongside more general measures such as the ones described earlier. However, they suggest that specific measures of accuracy are required for 'focussed tasks' that 'have been designed to elicit production of particular linguistic features (p.151.)

Two other areas of oral proficiency might also need to be considered if we are endeavouring to measure gain over a short period. One of these is pronunciation. This is quite challenging given the subjective nature of determining what is correct, what is correct but accented, and what is incorrect. However, with a group of learners from a particular language background, it should be possible to create an assessment grid for phonemes which cause problems for that group. The other area is lexical accuracy, which can be calculated as the number of clauses without lexical errors, or the number of lexical errors divided by the total number of words in the text (Skehan & Foster, 1997). Once more deciding what is incorrect is not straightforward. Skehan and Foster suggest that only errors where a word used is 'nonexistent in English or indisputably inappropriate' be counted (1997, p. 195). However, this is not always an easy decision when it comes to inappropriate collocations which may sound strange, but which we may feel are not definitively incorrect.

6. Conclusion

This paper has described some of the more common measures that have been used to assess modest changes in different aspects oral proficiency in non-native speakers. The discussion of this area has been fairly superficial, and there is clearly still much that we do not know. In particular, our understanding of just how the measures relate to each other and how they relate to overall progress in speaking competence is still quite limited. I think that at this stage we also need to remember that oral performance is a slippery phenomenon which can be affected by many uncontrollable variables and perhaps even certain unknown variables. At a given time, an individual's language will be less fluent or complex or accurate than at other times. The reasons for this may have nothing to do with the elicitation conditions, and may have very little to do with changes in the learners' underlying L2 language system or with their L2 skills development, but they might relate to the speaker's psychological or emotional state at the time of the elicitation. Low levels of fluency at the beginning of a Pre-Sessional course, for example, might simply be the result of higher levels of anxiety during the early days or a learner's tiredness caused by jetlag and the initial 'shock' of a new cultural and linguistic environment in which they find themselves. Nevertheless, bearing these caveats in mind, with groups of a reasonable size, it should be possible, using some of the measures described here, to identify mean gains in certain core aspects of oral proficiency over a 10 or 12 week period of intensive EAP study. The measures which seem to be the best candidates for this are: for fluency, production rate and mean length run; for complexity, number of clauses per 'T-unit' and number of words per 'T-unit'/per clause; for accuracy, number of error free 'T-units'/clauses. For studies focussing on interactive speech, rather than the 'T unit', consideration should be given to using the 'AS unit' as a unit of analysis.

Notes:

[1] At a recent BALEAP PIM meeting on the issue of rater-reliability in 2002, anecdotal experiences of problems with the reliability of the IELTS Speaking assessment were shared. One participant stated that they had come across a Japanese student who, tested in Japan, arrived in Britain with an IELTS speaking score of 8, but who was only considered to be at level 5 by the participant (Langley, 2002).

[2] Ellis & Barkhuizem (2005) explain that language can also be analysed in terms of its interactional complexity (eg the total number of turns performed by each speaker), its propositional complexity (e.g. the total number of major and minor ideas in the text), and in terms of its functional complexity (e.g. the total number of times a specific language function is used).

[3] Originally used by Hunt (1965) as a measure of children's syntactic maturity and defined as a 'minimal terminal unit' consisting of a main clause plus any

subordinating units, with subordinating clauses including all adverbial, adjectival and nominal clauses.

[4] 'A single speaker's utterance consisting of an independent clause or sub-clausal unit, together with any subordinate clauses associated with it' (Foster, Tonkyn & Wigglesworth, 2000, p. 365). In this scheme, an independent clause contains a finite verb, and a sub-clausal unit consists of a phrase which can be elaborated to a full clause by recovering its ellipted elements.

[5] Cooper (1976) defined two types of complex nominals: headed nominals (nouns plus adjectives or relative clauses), and non-headed-nominals (noun clauses, gerunds and infinitives).

[6] The standardised type/token ratio (STTR) is a mean score computed every n words as each text file is analysed. The default setting for n is 1000 words, but this can be changed so that it is possible to work with quite short sections of text.

References

Baddeley, A. (1986). *Working memory*. Oxford: Clarendon Press.

Brown, A. (1995). The effect of rater variables in the development of an occupation-specific language performance test. *Language Testing, 12,* 1-15.

Brown, A. (2005). *Interviewer variability in oral proficiency interviews*. Frankfurt am Main: Peter Lang.

Bygate, M. (1999). Quality of language and purpose of task: Patterns of learners' language on two oral communication tasks. *Language Teaching Research, 3,* 185-214.

Bygate, M. (2001). Effects of task repetition on the structure and control of oral language. In M. Bygate, P. Skehan & M. Swain (Eds.), *Researching pedagogic tasks: Second language learning, teaching and testing* (pp. 23-48). Harlow: Pearson Education.

Cooper, T. C. (1976). Measuring written syntactic patterns of second language learners of German. *The Journal of Educational Research, 69,* 176-183.

Dechert, H. W. & Raupach, M. (Eds.). (1980). *Temporal variables in speech: Studies in honour of Frieda Goldman-Eisler*. The Hague: Mouton Publishers.

Dyson, P. (1988). *The year abroad*. London: Central Bureau for Educational Visits and Exchanges.

Ejzenburg, R. (1992). *Understanding non-native fluency: The role of task structure and discourse variability.* Unpublished Ed.D dissertation, State University of New York.

Ellis, R. & Barkhuizen, G. (2005). *Analysing learner language.* Oxford: Oxford University Press.

Ellis, R. & Yuan, F. (2003). The effects of pre-task planning and on-line planning on fluency, complexity and accuracy in L2 monologic speech production. *Applied Linguistics, 24*, 1-27.

Ellis, R. & Yuan, F. (2005). The effects of careful within-task planning on oral and written task performance. In R. Ellis (Ed.*), Planning and task performance in a second language* (pp. 167-192). Amsterdam: John Benjamins Publishing Company.

Foster, P. & Skehan, P. (1996). The influence of planning and task type on second language performance. *Studies in Second Language Acquisition, 18,* 299-323.

Foster, P. & Skehan, P. (1999). The influence of source planning and focus of planning on task-based performance. *Language Teaching Research, 3,* 215-247.

Foster, P., Tonkyn, A. & Wigglesworth, G. (2000). Measuring spoken language: A unit for all reasons. *Applied Linguistics, 21*, 354 - 375.

Freed, B., Segalowitz, N. & Dewey, D. (2004). The concept of learning and the acquisition of French as an L2. *Studies in Second Language Acquisition, 26*, 275-301.

Goldman-Eisler, F. (1968). *Psycholinguistics: Experiments in spontaneous speech.* London, Academic Press.

Henry, K. (1996). Early L2 writing development: A study of autobiographical essays by university-level students of Russian. *Modern Language Journal, 80*, 309 - 326.

Hunt, K. W. (1965). *Grammatical structures written at three grade levels.* Urbana, IL: The National Council of Teachers of English.

Kawauchi, C. (2005). The effects of strategic planning on the oral narratives of learners with low and high intermediate L2 proficiency. In R. Ellis (Ed.*), Planning and task performance in a second language* (pp. 143-164). Amsterdam: John Benjamins Publishing Company.

Langley, G. (2002). Report from workshop on rater reliability. *BALEAP PIM Reports, 8.* Retrieved September 19th, 2006, from http://www.baleap.org.uk/pimreports/2002/soas/rater.htm

Larsen-Freeman, D. (1983). Assessing global second language proficiency. In H. W. Seliger & M. Long, (Eds.*), Classroom oriented research in second language acquisition* (pp. 287-304). Rowley, MA: Newbury House.

Levelt, W. (1989). *Speaking: From intention to articulation.* Cambridge, MA: MIT Press,

Möhle, D. (1984). A comparison of second language speech production of different native speakers. In H. W. Dechert, D. Möhle, & M. Raupach (Eds), *Second language productions* (pp. 26-49). Tubingen: Gunter Narr Verlag.

Riggenbach, H. (1991). Toward an understanding of fluency: A microanalysis of nonnative speaker conversations. *Discourse Processes, 14,* 423 - 441.

Scott, M. (2004*). Oxford WordSmith Tools, Version 4.0.* Oxford: Oxford University Press.

Segalowitz, N. & Freed, B. (2004). Context, contact, and cognition in oral fluency acquisition: Learning Spanish in at home and study abroad contexts. *Studies in Second Language Acquisition, 26,* 173 -199.

Sharma, A. (1980). Syntactic maturity: Assessing writing proficiency in a second language. In R. Silverstein (Ed.*), Occasional Papers in Linguistics, No 6* (pp. 318-325). Carbondale, IL: Southern Illinois University.

SIL (1996). *Speech analyzer: A speech analysis tool for Windows.* Summer Institute of Linguistics.

Skehan, P. (1996). Second language acquisition and task-based instruction. In , J. Willis & D. Willis (Eds.), *Challenge and change in language teaching* (pp. 17-30). Oxford: Heinemann.

Skehan, P. (1998). Task-based instruction. *Annual Review of Applied Linguistics, 18,* 268-286.

Skehan, P. (2001). Tasks and language performance assessment. In M. Bygate, P. Skehan, & M. Swain (Eds.), *Researching pedagogic tasks: second language learning teaching and testing* (pp. 167-185). Harlow: Pearson Education.

Skehan, P. & Foster, P. (1997). The influence of planning and post-task activities on accuracy and complexity in task based learning. *Language Teaching Research, 1,* 185-211.

Tonkyn, A. (2001). The many voices of fluency. Paper presented at BAAL Annual Meeting, Reading.

Towell, R., Hawkins, R. & Bazergui, N. (1996). The development of fluency in advanced learners of French. *Applied Linguistics, 17,* 84-119.

Wigglesworth, G. (1997). An investigation of planning time and proficiency level on oral test discourse. *Language Testing, 14,* 85-106.

Willis, F., Doble, G., Sankarayya, U. & Smithers, A. (1977). *Residence abroad and the student of modern languages: A preliminary survey.* Bradford: Modern Languages Centre, Bradford.

Wolfe-Quintero, K., Inagaki, I. & Kim, H. (1998). *Second language development in writing: Measures of fluency, accuracy and complexity.* Honolulu: University of Hawaii Second Language Teaching and Curriculum Center.

Yuan, F. & Ellis, R. (2003). The effects of pre-task planning and on-line planning on fluency, complexity and accuracy in L2 monologic oral production. *Applied Linguistics, 24,* 1-27.

Establishing the effectiveness of EAP writing programmes for Chinese undergraduates

Simon Kinzley, University of Lancaster

Abstract

This paper reports on aspects of a study that tracks students from the beginning of a university Pre-Sessional course through to the end of their second term of study for an undergraduate degree in Media and Cultural Studies. The study is primarily concerned with whether these students adopt the practices of academic writing advocated on the Pre-Sessional course once they have actually begun their degrees and also considers whether there is a link between adoption of these practices and academic success. In this paper, I concentrate on the methods used for conducting this research; their strengths and possible flaws.

1. Introduction

Determining whether EAP programmes improve the academic performance of overseas students in UK universities requires that we answer three questions:

1. Which components of these programmes represent an innovation to these students, i.e. something new that they did not already know or apply to their work before studying it on an EAP course?
2. Once these students leave their EAP courses and proceed onto their degree programmes, do they apply the practices they learned in EAP to their "real" studies?
3. Is there a positive relationship between the adoption of the study practices taught on EAP courses and the achievement of good academic results once the students begin their actual degree programmes? In other words, do the students who understand and follow our advice achieve better results than those who do not?

If we intend to apply the information gained by answering these questions to the implementation of continuous improvement of EAP programmes, then we must also ask *why* the answers to questions two and three are as they are.

In this paper I attempt to show how we can answer the questions outlined above. I begin by introducing innovation theory and explaining its usefulness for analysing and answering these questions. Next, I introduce the epistemological basis of my analysis and outline the specific data gathering techniques I use and relate them to all of the above. Finally, I discuss how this approach can be related to wider methodologies in educational research and how this might be applied to building a wider picture of the effectiveness of EAP across a number of different programmes being delivered throughout the UK and beyond.

2. A brief introduction to innovation theory, its applications to language education and language learners

Innovation involves conscious, overt and fundamental behaviour change in the implementation of an activity in a social system (Chin & Benne, 1976; Markee, 1993; Markee, 1997; Miles, 1964; Nichols, 1983; Rogers & Shoemaker, 1971; Rogers, 2003; Stoller, 1994; West & Farr, 1990). To this has been added that this way of acting should either be new or subjectively perceived as new by participants in the change (Markee, 1997; Rogers, 2003).

The aim of innovations is to achieve *adoption*. Adoption 'is a decision to make full use of a new idea as the best course of action available' (Rogers & Shoemaker, 1971, p. 26). Adoption requires *diffusion*. Diffusion 'is the process by which innovations spread to members of a social system' (Markee, 1993, p. 12). Diffusion is achieved by *communication*: 'the process through which messages are transferred from a source to a receiver' (Rogers & Shoemaker, 1971, p. 11) and manifested through *implementation*: 'the process of putting into practice an idea, programme or set of activities and structures new to the people attempting or expected to change' (Fullan, 2001, p. 69).

2.1. Innovation in education

Educational innovation mainly concerns changes in *materials*, *skills/approaches* and *beliefs/values* (Fullan, 2001; Henrichsen, 1989; Markee, 1987; Stoller, 1994). Generally the authors named above discuss innovation in relation to professionals. Henrichsen and Fullan, though, do also acknowledge a place for the analysis of its impact on learners.

Markee describes the value of applying an innovation perspective to change in language education as follows:

> ...a 'diffusion-of-innovations' perspective on syllabus design provides curriculum specialists, materials developers, and teachers with a coherent set of guiding principles for the development and implementation of

language teaching innovations. Furthermore, it supplies evaluators with criteria for retrospective evaluations of the extent to which these innovations have actually been implemented. In other words, this perspective provides a unified framework for conceptualising both the development and evaluation of innovations in language teaching (1993, p. 229).

These conceptualisations of *development* and *evaluation* offer promising frameworks for analysing the extent to which overseas students have adopted the study practices advocated on EAP courses and for probing the reasons for these outcomes.

I now look at what the theory reveals about how innovations proceed from design through to sustainable implementation. I hope that this will clarify the elements of successful innovation, so that later these can provide a framework that will be helpful for researchers seeking to determine whether EAP programmes have actually led to successful learning outcomes among overseas students.

2.2. The innovation process

The innovation process is often understood in terms of answering the following question: *Who adopts what, where, when, why* and *how*? (Cooper, 1982, 1989; Markee, 1997). I now discuss each of these in turn.

2.2.1. Who

Who refers to the social roles played by different stakeholders in an innovation (Markee, 1993, 1997). Markee (1997, chap. 4) provides the following role categories: *adopters, suppliers, implementers, entrepreneurs* and *clients*. *Adopters* decide whether an innovation should be developed. *Suppliers* design it. *Implementers* put it into practice. *Entrepreneurs* - also known as change agents - oversee design process. *Clients* are the intended beneficiaries of the innovation.

Another actor who may be present in the process is called a *resister*. A resister is somebody who opposes an innovation (Markee, 1997, p. 44). The importance of resisters and resistance in innovation theory should not be understated because as Adams and Chen (1981) note, three quarters of innovations fail over time.

Markee (1997) states that these roles are not mutually exclusive and participants in the innovation process may play more than one role simultaneously. I illustrate this in relation to the Lancaster University Pre-Sessional course where I am conducting my own research:

Adopters include those in the Lancaster University Linguistics Department responsible for determining funding for research and development of the Pre-Sessional course and course managers (past and present).

Suppliers include course managers (past and present), researchers and teachers.

Implementers include course managers (present), teachers, secretaries and students.

Entrepreneurs include course managers (past and present) and researchers.

Clients include students, Lancaster University academic departments receiving our students and (perhaps) teachers.

The relationships are further complicated when people do more than one job. I, for example, am a researcher, a manager and a teacher on the Pre-Sessional course.

Beretta (1990), by implication, illustrates a deficiency in this part of Markee's framework. In an analysis of implementation among teaching staff of Prabhu's procedural syllabus he found that the most significant barrier to adoption among teachers was not a lack of willingness, but rather a lack of expertise. The result was that Beretta identified levels of partial adoption amongst some teachers; something that falls between adoption and resistance. Since we hypothesise that students' grades are differentiated, at least in part, by how well they implement the notions of good academic practice that we introduce them to, it is clear that an extra category of stakeholder is required for this kind of research; someone who may have the will or potential, but not yet the capability to adopt or implement an innovation. I shall call this person an *apprentice.*

Finally, it is important to note that there is a lack of analysis regarding the role of the student in innovation. Rectifying this problem is important for two reasons.

First, as Shamim (1996) notes, learner resistance can hinder adoption.

Second, Fullan (2001) argues that failure to include students in the process of innovation goes against current thought in both cognitive science and sociology regarding how to improve educational outcomes for students. His description of the current beliefs in cognitive science seems to match almost perfectly much what is said about the skills of process writing and learner autonomy that EAP aims to develop:

> ....traditionally, teaching has "focused too narrowly on the memorisation of information, giving short shrift to critical thinking, conceptual understanding, and in-depth knowledge of subject matter" (National Research Council [NRC], 1999, p. 25). Teaching and learning for deep understanding (which means learners can critically apply what they know to comprehending and addressing new problems and situations) has now become the goal of this new and radical pedagogy (Bransford et al., 1999; Gardner, 1999). (Fullan, 2001, p. 152).

He then explains how sociologists have argued that encouraging students to develop the independent and autonomous practices requires a blurring of the boundaries and a diminishing of the authoritarian relationship between teachers and learners (Fullan, 2001).

> The new common ground for both cognitive scientists and sociologists concerns *motivation and relationships*, that is, it is only when schooling operates in a way that connects students relationally in a relevant, engaging, and worthwhile experience that substantial learning will occur...the main problem with disengaged students is that they lack a meaningful personal connection with teachers and others in the school; in other words, they lack the motivational capacity to become involved in learning. Incidentally, this is why emotional development for children must go hand-in-hand with cognitive development (Fullan, 2001, p. 152).

Consequently, studying learner adoption behaviours regarding changes we ask them to undertake on our own EAP courses contributes not only to these programmes' further development, but also to our understanding of how to account for the student in the wider theory and planning of educational innovations in general.

2.2.2. Adopts

This concerns the decision making processes of potential adopters (Fullan, 2001; Markee, 1997; Rogers, 2003; Rogers and Shoemaker, 1971). Rogers (2003) names five stages of adoption. These are: '1) gaining knowledge about an innovation, 2) being persuaded of its value, 3) making a preliminary decision to adopt the innovation, 4) implementing their decision to adopt, and 5) confirming their decision to continue using the innovation' (p. 323). Fullan (2001, p. 50) names four stages: *initiation, implementation, continuation* and *outcome*.

Using my research as an example, Rogers's concept of *gaining knowledge* would refer to students' introduction to the innovation (academic writing practices) in the classroom. Rogers's concepts of *persuasion* and *preliminary decision* match Fullan's notion of *initiation* and would refer to students' preliminary decision to try the writing practices. *Implementation*, a term used by both authors, would involve an initial phase of students applying the writing practices to their work. Rogers's notion of *confirmation* and Fullan's of *continuation* would relate to the students' decision to keep implementing the writing practices throughout their degree studies. Fullan's concept of *outcomes* would represent the essays written and the results achieved.

By comparing relative levels of adoption among different members of my research population, I hope this concept of *outcomes* will help in determining whether higher levels of adoption result in higher levels of academic achievement.

2.2.3. What

According to Markee (1997), *what* defines the innovation itself.

Fullan describes innovation as being "multidimensional" (2001, p. 39).

> There are at least three components or dimensions at stake in implementing any new programme or policy: (1) the possible use of new or revised *materials* (instructional resources such as curriculum materials or technologies), (2) the possible use of new teaching approaches, and (3) the possible alteration of *beliefs* (e.g., pedagogical assumptions and theories underlying particular new policies or programmes) (Fullan, 2001, p. 39).

From this perspective, innovation can be seen as a form of development. Markee, in fact, goes so far as to describe development and innovation as being synonymous (1997, p. 51). This would certainly seem to match the innovation decision process I describe in Section 2.2.2 that takes adopters from gaining knowledge of an innovation through to learning outcomes. And this in turn matches many of the ideals presented as core objectives of EAP writing courses, such as becoming adept at synthesising, analysing in a critical manner, constructing a reasoned argument, evaluating, thinking logically, drawing conclusions and adopting the processes of self-managed learning.

However, in determining the nature of innovation, it is also important to acknowledge that there are at least three pitfalls.

First, it cannot be assumed without evidence that something is an innovation. In this article, I have so far presented academic writing skills as if they are an innovation, but I have not yet presented any evidence to support this assumption.

Second, Markee notes that '...change may be necessary, but it is psychologically unsettling' (1997, p. 53). He gives the example of language learners in a communicative classroom:

As language learners acquire "communicative innovations...they must be able to tolerate potentially high levels of affective ambiguity whenever their interlanguage is destabilised" (1997, p. 52).

While the desired outcome is for learners to '...transcend their initial feelings of incompetence and move on to higher levels of professional [in this research, learner] sophistication and performance' (Markee, 1997, p. 53), the anxiety generated may mean that, instead, students fail to achieve this.

Third, just because something is an innovation, does not mean that it can be assumed to benefit its intended recipients. For example, Markee cites Brumfit's (1981) attack on the notional syllabus for denying learners the generative grammar necessary to autonomously construct their own sentences (1997, p. 46). Such pitfalls have several implications for the conduct of research into the beneficial effects of EAP.

First, as a starting point, this research must determine to what extent EAP courses represent innovations to learners by establishing which processes and products really are new to members of the target population.

Second, in trying to determine the reasons for students' adoption behaviours, I must give consideration to whether adopting new practices does in every instance create anxiety that in turn leads to resistance.

Third, by answering the question of whether higher rates of adoption result in higher levels of academic achievement, I hope to answer the question of whether the innovation is beneficial.

2.2.4. Where

Where is generally used to refer to the socio-cultural context of an innovation rather than its geographical location (Markee, 1997, p. 55). For example, Kennedy (1988, p. 332) describes a hierarchy of concentric circles descending from the all-encompassing cultural through to the political, administrative, educational, institutional down to classroom innovation.

2.2.5. When

When describes the relationship between time elapsed and the number of users adopting an innovation in a social system (Markee, 1997, p. 43; Rogers & Shoemaker, 1971). Markee argues that: 'we can quantify diffusion as the *percentage* of adopters in a social system who adopt an innovation in a given period of *time*' (1997, p. 57). Linked to this Rogers and Shoemaker go so far as to attribute individuals with adopter categories based on the speed at which they adopt and use this as a basis for calculating when diffusion has occurred (1971, chap. 5).

2.2.6. Why

Why concerns '…the psychological profiles of different adopter types and discusses the attributes that successful innovations possess' (Markee, 1997, p. 43).

2.2.7. How

How concerns the"different approaches to effecting change" (Markee, 1997, p. 43).

3. Epistemology and methodology

Developing a framework capable of producing generalisable research methods potentially applicable to the analysis of all EAP programmes requires two further questions to be addressed:

1. How can general theory as discussed in Section 2 be applied to research into EAP learners in a particular situation?
2. How can research into EAP learners in a particular situation inform our understanding of the effectiveness of EAP programmes in general?

Behind both questions lies a deeper enquiry: How is it possible to ensure that conclusions are based on a correct interpretation of the evidence or that the evidence is both sufficient and accurate? Addressing this question requires an analysis of causality.

3.1. Causality

Causality studies how factors or events lead to consequences over time (Miles & Huberman, 1994, p. 145). In short, it relates evidence to conclusions. Since the aim is to prove whether or not an innovation (in this case an EAP programme) has lead to changes in the behaviour of intended beneficiaries (here, learners), an understanding of causality is fundamental.

Miles and Huberman identify five types of causality (1994, pp. 146-147):

First, *local emphasis* – This limits analysis of cause and effect to what is practical and useful.

> We can speculate about…distant factors, but if they have an effect, it is here and now. The immediate causal nexus in front of us: A teacher felt, said or did something, and then several students felt, said or did something over a period of time…we must be concerned with the validity of our findings in a *particular* setting by achieving thorough local acquaintance (1994, p. 146).

Second, *causal complexity* - Miles and Huberman argue that in social science we can rarely see single causes leading to single effects and instead must probe complex *causal networks* because: 'The causes are not only multiple, but "conjunctural" - they combine and effect each other as well as the effects. Furthermore, effects of multiple causes are not the same in all contexts, and different combinations of causes can turn out to have similar effects' (Miles & Huberman, 1994, p. 146).

Third, *temporality* - This concerns seeing the progression of events as being like "plots" moving forwards through time (Miles & Huberman, 1994, p. 147).

Fourth, *retrospection* - Research always requires looking back at previous events to find models. We cannot, for example, report on research findings until we get results (1994).

Fifth, *variables and processes* - Analysing data and identifying the generalised categories they occupy (identified as variables) and examining their interactions (processes) (1994).

These five processes can combine into *causal networks* showing: '...the most important independent and dependent variables in a field study and the relationships among them...The plot of these relationships is directional, rather than solely correlational' (1994, p. 153).

Miles and Huberman identify two ways of building causal networks: *inductive* and *deductive*.

The inductive approach, also known at the *constructive* or *generative,* is where:

> ...the researcher discovers recurrent phenomena in the stream of local experience and finds recurrent relations among them. These working hypotheses are modified and refined progressively in the next fieldwork pass. The local cause map emerges piecemeal and inductively. It has regularity and pattern; some things happen only when others do or don't. These things and the links between them acquire their own names or labels, cluster into probable causes and the effects they appear to engender - and the analyst has a causal network (1994, p. 155).

The deductive approach, also known as the *enumerative* or *conceptual,* is one in which: '...the researcher has some orienting constructs or propositions to test or observe in the field. These analytic units are operationalised and then matched with a body of field data' (Miles & Huberman, 1994, p. 155).

The difference is that deductive researchers begin with a model and inductive researchers end with one. Either way, the model is refined throughout a project according to data discovered so that the relationship can be seen as a process of dialogue rather than of mutual exclusion. Effectively, employing both the inductive and deductive models concurrently facilitates cross-checking of a framework.

3.2. Henrichsen's Hybrid Model

In my discussion of causal networks I identified deductive models as useful for providing orienting models or constructs to categorise and process real-world data.

In my own research I use a model known as *Henrichsen's Hybrid Model*. Here, I briefly describe and relate it to my own research. This is first to demonstrate how wider general theory informs my research and, second, so that in Sections 3.3 and 3.4, I can show, by way of example, how these research methods cover my own area of study.

3.2.1. Antecedents

Antecedents are the historical and cultural background that an existing tradition of teaching and learning has grown out of (Henrichsen, 1989, p. 79). Henrichsen states these consist of four factors: *Characteristics of the intended user system*; *characteristics of the intended users of the innovation*; *established pedagogical practices*; and *experiences of previous reformers*.

Characteristics of the intended user system are, according to Henrichsen, 'the nature of the school system and of the society in which those are found' (1989, p. 79). This means the academic department that the students I am studying entered once they completed the Lancaster University Pre-Sessional course.

Characteristics of intended users of the innovation are the recipients' 'attitudes, values, norms and abilities [that] strongly influence the course of a diffusion/implementation effort' (Henrichsen, 1989, p. 80). This means the characteristics of the students whose adoption behaviours I am studying.

Traditional pedagogical practices are the long established practices of teaching and learning that intended adopters have experienced and are most familiar with (1989, p. 81). I have decided, instead, to refer to *established pedagogical practices* because some of the educational environments I consider here are relatively modern. This means the teaching environments in which my research population studied in their country of origin.

Experiences of previous reformers are 'the experiences of earlier reform efforts in the same (or a similar) socio-cultural context' (Henrichsen, 1989, p. 81). These refer to the experiences of previous designers and managers of the Lancaster University Pre-Sessional course.

3.2.2. Processes

Processes are factors influencing the change process towards adopting or rejecting an innovation (Henrichsen, 1989, p. 81). These are divided into five categories: *source, message, plans and strategies, channels of communication, receiver* and *factors which facilitate/hinder change.*

Source means the innovator (1989, p. 80). This refers to the designers of the Lancaster University academic writing Pre-Sessional course.

Message means the innovation (1989, p. 80). This refers to the Lancaster University Pre-Sessional academic writing course.

Plans and strategies are factors accounted for in attempts to ensure diffusion of an innovation (1989, p. 82). These refer to methods put in place to encourage diffusion of the academic writing practices advocated on the Lancaster University Pre-Sessional academic writing course.

Channels of communication are methods of explaining an innovation to prospective adopters. These refer to ways of delivering the Lancaster University Pre-Sessional academic writing course.

Receiver factors relate to *awareness, interest* and *evaluation* stages of the innovation decision process (1989, p. 80). These refer to the decision processes the students in my research population go through during the Lancaster University Pre-Sessional academic writing course.

Factors that hinder/facilitate change are attributes of the innovation itself, of the resource system delivering it, of the intended user system and inter-elemental factors (relationships between the other elements involved in the diffusion process (1989, p. 92) that are either positively or negatively related to adoption. These will be described in the context of the Lancaster University Pre-Sessional academic writing course.

3.2.3. Consequences

Consequences are the outcomes of an innovation process (Henrichsen, 1989, p. 94). These are *adoption, rejection, confirmation, continuation, discontinuation, later adoption* and *continued rejection*.

Adoption means use of an innovation in the form intended by a change agent. This will refer to adoption by the students in my research population.

Rejection is the decision not to use an innovation. This refers to any instances of rejection by students in my research population.

Confirmation is the recipient's final adoption or rejection decision. This can be either to keep using an innovation already adopted (continuation); to stop using an innovation that was initially adopted (discontinuation); to adopt an innovation that was initially rejected (later adoption) or to confirm an original decision to reject an innovation (continued rejection) (1989, p. 80). These refer to confirmation decisions by students in my research population.

Having shown how I can apply a deductive model to demarcate my research area I now discuss the strategies I employ to maximise my ability to gather credible data that covers this area.

3.3. Data gathering strategies

In determining how to gather data for the inductive part of my research I plan to apply two strategies: *triangulation* and *intensive/extensive research methods*.

3.3.1. Triangulation

Triangulation is: 'the use of two or more methods of data collection in the study of some aspect of human behaviour' (Cohen & Manion, 1997, p. 233). It is useful for five reasons.

First, when several methods of analysis are used to answer the same research question they can 'enable confirmation or corroboration of each other' (Miles & Huberman, 1994, p. 141).

Second, multiple methods help 'elaborate or develop analysis, providing richer detail' (Miles & Huberman, 1994, p. 141).

Third, in instances where the findings of varying research methods are not identical, identification of this issue allows the researcher to: 'initiate new lines of thinking through attention to surprises or paradoxes, "turning ideas around", providing fresh insight' (Miles & Huberman, 1994, p. 141).

Fourth, triangulation can be used to reduce or at least account for artefacts of method. For example, interviewing students about their approach to study could cause them to consciously reflect on the subject in ways that they otherwise would not have done. This would leave the question unclear as to whether the work they produce is entirely the result of previous educational input or has been partially influenced by participating in an interview. In such a situation findings could be triangulated by comparing the performance of students who participated in the interviews with that of students who did not to see if there were any detectable differences in the performance of the two groups.

Fifth, triangulation can be used to help identify observer-induced artefacts i.e. bias or misunderstanding of a particular researcher resulting in a distorted interpretation of the data.

Cohen & Manion identify six different types of triangulation:

1. Methodological triangulation: (a) same method on different occasions (b) different methods on same object
2. Time triangulation - Takes a longitudinal view cross-checking through more than one time period; accounts for social change and time related processes
3. Space triangulation - Attempts to overcome limitations which may result from studies only being undertaken in one culture or subculture
4. Combined levels of triangulation - Levels of the individual, the group and the society
5. Theoretical triangulation - In methods (more than one study using the same method), between methods (using more than one method to undertake a study)

6. Investigator triangulation – more than one observer is utilised on a study (1997, p. 236)

3.3.2. Intensive and extensive social research

Sayer (2000, p. 23-24) illustrates these concepts by describing the idea of two groups of Martians coming to Earth and encountering human beings for the first time. One would analyse the body of a human *intensively*, the other *extensively*. The intensive group would concentrate on one part of the body and analyse all the areas connected to it to a certain depth. The extensive group would look at the entire body, but only superficially. Both might draw different conclusions about the nature of the human body and would therefore find each other's analysis helpful in verifying and clarifying certain issues.

This can be described as another example of methodological triangulation. However, its distinctiveness as a strategy is its logistical advantages. I lack the resources to intensively research every area demarcated by the Henrichsen's Hybrid Model. It was not, for example, possible to conduct research in the home country of my research population. This means I cannot investigate matters such as *established pedagogical practices* as intensively as I would like.

3.4. Research methods

Primarily my research will be a case study incorporating a longitudinal/developmental perspective, supplemented with some historical study.

3.4.1. The case study

Case studies observe:

> ...the characteristics of an individual unit – a child, a clique, a class, a school or a community. The purpose of such observation is to probe deeply and to analyse intensively the multifarious phenomena that constitute the life cycle of the unit with a view to establishing generalisations about the wider population to which that unit belongs (Cohen & Manion, 1997, p. 106-7).

The unit under study is the 2005-6 cohort of students from partner universities in China studying for undergraduate degrees in Media and Cultural Studies at Lancaster University on a 2+2 programme (known as: PRC 2+2 BA MACS).

This study is developmental/longitudinal in that it aims to describe relationships between a set of variables and changes in those relationships 'as a function of time' (Cohen & Manion, 1997, p. 67). In education this approach to research is considered valuable because it can be used to trace the development of learning (p. 68). Similarly, it is logical to argue that it is also useful for tracing the innovation decision process.

3.4.1.1. Method

I have interviewed nine members of the 2005-6 cohort of PRC 2+2 BA MACS students four times each. I did this at the beginning of the Pre-Sessional course, at the end of the Pre-Sessional course, at the beginning of Term 2 and at the end of Term 3. I also intend to do a content analysis of all of the essays they wrote during this period as well as the feedback on them received from tutors on the Pre-Sessional course and lecturers in the Media and Cultural Studies department. Finally, I have interviewed one lecturer each from all of the three core courses that these students must submit work for during the first year at Lancaster University.

3.4.1.2. Research questions addressed

1. What aspects of the Lancaster University Pre-Sessional academic writing course constitute an innovation for these students?
2. To what extent do PRC 2+2 BA MACS students adopt the models of academic writing advocated on the Lancaster University Pre-Sessional course?
3. What characteristics of these models do these students adopt, fail to adopt or reject?
4. How can we explain these students' adoption behaviours?
5. Do higher rates of adoption necessarily result in higher levels of academic achievement? Why/why not?

3.4.1.3. Linkage zone

The *message, plans and strategies* and *channels of communication* categories of the linkage model can be covered in the case study by interviews with the designers of the Pre-Sessional course and content analysis of the Pre-Sessional course syllabus and essay feedback given to students during the programme.

Discussion of *awareness, interest* and *evaluation* of the innovation can be undertaken through interviews with the students themselves as well as by looking at their written output.

Factors that facilitate/hinder change are addressed by interviews with students, course designers for the Pre-Sessional, in-Sessional and BA MACS courses and BA MACS lecturers.

Interviews with 2+2 BA MACS students; EAP tutors and course designers and Media and Cultural Studies lecturers triangulate all of the *consequences* described by Henrichsen's model: i.e. *adoption, rejection, confirmation, continuation, discontinuation, later adoption* and *continued rejection*. This should be further cross-referenced by referring to students' degree essays.

3.4.1.4. Methods of triangulation

The case study data triangulates with the historical study relating the content of interviews with staff and students, to documentation describing the *characteristics of the intended user system*, the *characteristics of intended users of the innovation* and *traditional pedagogical practices*.

The *content analysis* of student essays triangulates with the student, teacher and lecturer interviews by enabling comparison between statements about academic writing, samples of academic writing, feedback and grades produced throughout the Pre-Sessional course and Terms 1 and 2 of the first year of the Lancaster University segment of the BA MACS two-plus-two degree programme.

Lecturer interviews can be triangulated with other lecturer interviews and also with student interviews. Students' interviews triangulate in the same way and also through time since each student will be interviewed on four occasions throughout the period of the study.

3.4.1.5. Evidence of causality

Local emphasis is accounted for because interviewees are being asked about their responses to experiences in their immediate environment.

Simon Kinzley

Causal complexities will be uncovered as a result of the scope of the hybrid model covered in the interviews and also as a result of the multiple methods of triangulation

Temporal causality can be considered as a result of the longitudinal nature of the study.

Coding and, where necessary, transcribing the case study data provide an opportunity to identify causal *variables and processes* relevant to the questions being researched.

3.4.2. Historical research

Historical research is 'systematic and objective location, evaluation and synthesis of evidence in order to establish facts and draw conclusions about past events' (Cohen & Manion, 1997, p. 45).

3.4.2.1. Method

The aim of this part of my research is to establish extensively the *who, what, where* and *when* of the antecedents of the Pre-Sessional course with regard to my research population.

The historical aspect of the project will mostly concern the collection of *primary data*. This is defined as: (a) the relics of a given period, and (b) items that have a direct relationship with the events being reconstructed (Cohen & Manion, 1997, p. 50). However, some secondary data will also be gathered regarding the history of language education in China.

Specifically, I will undertake the following investigations:

1. Analysis of written material relating to the history of Chinese education in general and English language education in particular
2. Analysis of any written material available that describes something of the history of the institutions participating in the Lancaster University Chinese university partner project
3. Analysis of materials and syllabi used for delivery of the Chinese segment of the two-plus-two BA MACS courses
4. Analysis of the 2+2 staff handbook for China

5. Interviews with designers of in-Sessional support courses for 2+2 BA MACS students
6. Interviews with the students themselves that include coverage of their past language learning experiences in China

3.4.2.2. Research questions addressed

My aim here is consider cultural and historical causes of student adoption behaviours.

3.4.2.3. Linkage zone

The *intended user system* will be addressed by interviews with designers and teachers of the in-Sessional support course delivered to 2+2 BA MACS students studying at Lancaster University and from interviews with the students themselves.

The *intended users of the innovation* will be addressed by interviews with the students.

Established pedagogical practices will be addressed by: analysis of the history of Chinese English language education; analysis of the syllabi used for two-plus-two study in China; analysis of documentation relating to the delivery of the 2+2 programme between the participating university partners; interviews with the students themselves.

Experiences of previous reformers and *source* will be analysed by interviewing designers of the Pre-Sessional course.

3.4.2.4. Method of triangulation

Interviews can be used to triangulate data by: comparing the comments of course designers with each other and with students; comparing the comments of students with each other as well as with the course designers; the comments of course designers and students with all of the documentation used in the historical analysis of the innovation's antecedents.

The *case study* will triangulate with the methods used in the historical study by comparing observations of student performance and reactions in the Pre-

Sessional course with those anticipated from the data previously gathered on the antecedents.

3.4.2.5. Evidence of causality

I address *causal complexity* by examining all of the categories of antecedents outlined in Henrichsen's model from perspectives provided by historical documentation as well as interviews with students and course designers.

The historical method provides the first component of a view of *temporality* within the data by providing an account of what happened prior to students experiencing the innovation itself. This also provides an opportunity to examine the *retrospective* aspects of causality.

The *inductive* element of this part of the research arises from an attempt to build the data up into a coherent generalisable model of the experience being studied.

The *deductive* element of this part of the research will arise from an attempt to fit all of the data gathered into the categories provided by Henrichsen's linkage model.

4. Conclusion

In this paper I have attempted to identify the key questions that must be answered if we are to determine whether EAP programmes can be considered effective. I have also tried to demonstrate how innovation theory combined with appropriate methods of gathering and interpreting data can be used to answer these questions in relation to a single EAP programme. While I cannot claim that this research will necessarily yield findings applicable to all EAP programmes everywhere, I think that the methods outlined here may be of use to researchers elsewhere and that, if they are, the interlocking findings of a number of investigations may be helpful in building a body of evidence that will assist in making wider generalisations about the EAP teaching process possible.

References

Adams, R. S. & Chen, D. (1981). *The process on educational innovation: An international perspective*. London: Kogan Page/UNESCO Press.

Beretta, A. (1990). Implementation of the Bangalore project. *Applied Linguistics, 11*, 321-337.

Brumfit, C. J. (1981). Notional syllabuses revisited: A response. *Applied Linguistics, 2*, 90-92.

Chin, R. A. B. &. Benne, K. D. (1976). General strategies for effecting changes in human systems. In R. A. B. Chin & K. D. Benne (Eds.), *The planning of change*. New York: Holt, Rinehart and Winston.

Cohen, L. & Manion, L. (1994). *Research methods in education*. New York: Routledge.

Cooper, R. L. (1982). A framework for the study of language spread. In R. L. Cooper (Ed.), *Language spread: Studies in diffusion and social change* (pp. 5-36). Bloomington: Indiana University Press and Washington D.C.: Center for Applied Linguistics.

Cooper, R. L. (1989). *Language planning and social change*. Cambridge: Cambridge University Press.

Fullan, M. (2001). *The new meaning of educational change*. London: Routledge Farmer.

Henrichsen, E. L. (1989). *Diffusion of innovations in language teaching: The ELEC effort in Japan 1956-1968*. Westport, CT: Greenwood Press.

Kennedy, C. (1988). Evaluation of the management of change in ELT projects. *Applied Linguistics, 9*, 329-42.

Markee, N. (1993). The diffusion of innovation in language teaching. *Annual Review of Applied Linguistics, 13*, 229-243.

Markee, N. (1997). *Managing curricular innovation*. Cambridge: Cambridge University Press.

Miles, M. B. (1964). *Innovation in education*. New York: Teachers College, Columbia University.

Miles, M. B. & Huberman, A. M. (1994). *Qualitative data analysis*. London: Sage.

Nicholls, A. (1983). *Managing educational innovations*. London: Allen and Unwin.

Rogers, E. M., with F. F. Shoemaker (1971). *Communication of innovations: A cross-cultural approach*. New York: Free Press.

Rogers, E. M. (2003). *Diffusion of innovations*. New York: Free Press.

Sayer, A. (2000). *Realism and social science*. London: Sage.

Shamim, F. (1996). Learner resistance to innovation in classroom methodology. In H. Coleman (Ed.), *Society and the language classroom* (pp. 105–121). Cambridge: Cambridge University Press.

Stoller, F. L. (1994). The diffusion of innovations in intensive ESL programmes. *Applied Linguistics, 15*, 300-327.

West, M. A. & Farr, J. L. (1990). *Innovation and creativity at work: Psychological and organisational strategies.* New York: Wiley.

Does EAP work? A personal view

Sonya Saunders, Royal Holloway, University of London

1. Introduction

What seems like a fairly simple question actually turns out to be a very complex one. Basically three further questions immediately arose in my mind which were:

- How can we find out?

- Can we prove it?

- Do we need to prove it?

Then a reality check set in - if we EAP teachers cannot prove it, could we be out of a job? Perhaps that is a little melodramatic, but with people increasingly trying to make their work more "scientific" and "objective" as a justification for doing it, perhaps the question should be investigated by research.

2. A failed attempt at some research

What my colleague and I originally proposed was as follows:

- This paper will present data which examines the extent to which attendance on a Pre-Sessional and/or a one year foundation programme actually translated into academic success on a Master's course for a group of management students in 2004/5.

- Although all students entered the Master's programme with comparable IELTS bands, the degree to which these students had been exposed to EAP varied significantly. Did students who had attended courses focusing on, for example, extended writing skills, seminar/presentation skills, critical reading and listening skills achieve a higher graduation rate?

The research failed for the following reasons:

- The University would not release the necessary data.

- The variables are probably too many to make this a valid piece of research

- The research would probably benefit from long-term involvement rather than the "hindsight" that this proposal indicates.

So why is this apparently simple question so difficult to answer? Several people

110

pulled out of making presentations at the BALEAP PIM on this question, probably because, like me, they thought they could show empirically that EAP works, but for several reasons they have not been able to acquire the data.

I believe that some reasons might be:

- Under privacy laws, universities may feel that they do not need to give out information on whether students have been successful or not.
- Universities most likely do not want to disclose failure.
- Even if EAP courses are apparently successful, many other factors could influence students' success or failure - ranging from personal reasons to poor/inspiring teaching or to overly easy/difficult examination structures.

Perhaps first of all we need to look at what exactly EAP is, and then decide if it is measurable in itself. Then we might ask how EAP and/or Study Skills are related. This brought up a host of other questions:

- Are they the same or different?
- How much of what we teach is Study Skills and how much is language?
- Is EAP a combination of English and Study Skills?
- Might we say that "English" is the language part of it and "Academic Purposes" is the study skills aspect of what we do, or is this too simplistic?
- How do we measure the above elements?

Then the question arose "What does the word 'work' in the title "Does EAP work" mean? 'Work,' even in this context, is a very general word and could mean several things. Does it mean that students who have taken EAP courses have done better than those who did not? Is it something that is measurable and if so how do we measure this? What if some students were:

- better/worse at English despite IELTS scores,
- good/poor at their subject which affected their final result,
- exposed to inspiring/uninspiring teaching,
- affected by other variables such as illness or something else which caused them to miss classes.

So what evidence could we use to show whether EAP works or not? I think there are four ways, none of which are totally satisfactory, that we often try to give as evidence to answer the question. First of all is anecdotal evidence which we get from anywhere and everywhere, and this is what we language teachers use most of the time. Secondly, there are student views, but how can they judge whether EAP works or not, particularly when they do not have an overview of their success until after they have finished their degrees. Thirdly are the views of academic departments in colleges and universities, where it seems to me that they often have preconceived ideas about language teaching, and sometimes no real knowledge about the idea that other cultures do not always understand our academic traditions. Fourthly are the personal views of tutors/lecturers of EAP, where I think we have gut feelings that it must work, or how do we justify our existence? But are any of these sources real evidence?

I will look at these four sources in more detail. Anecdotal evidence is something we tend to use a great deal of the time. We may feel that we can see our students success. An example could be that during a one year specialised EAP course we can see overall improvement in IELTS scores if students come in with one score, and improve it once or twice more over the year. But this does not definitely prove that it is EAP that has improved their IELTS results. They might improve just as well if the students did a general English language improvement course, or even no course at all. According to my colleague at Royal Holloway, Sophia Stavrakakis, "What we are probably doing is accelerating students' acclimatisation to UK academic expectations."

When thinking about students views, generally, even when student course evaluation questionnaires are given anonymously, students tend to be positive about what they have done. Questionnaires sent to last years pre Master's students all agreed that the EAP courses had been useful. But I do not know those students' Master's results. It is probably very hard for students to be objective, particularly before they have an overall picture of how they have performed in their academic subjects.

Academic department's views are hard to gauge mainly because they sometimes work backwards. They may wait until a student is failing then expect language teachers to make it "right". Admissions also often allow students into departments with low English levels for a host of reasons, probably most of them financial. Individually some academic lecturers might have no real understanding of other cultures, and may have an expectation that if students are coming to the UK to study they should know how to do what is expected of UK students. PhD students often suffer most for this reason as they may have first and second degrees from their own countries which are very distinguished, but have no real clue of what is expected of them here in the UK.

Then there are our own views as EAP Lecturers/Tutors/Teaching Fellows of EAP. We probably feel that it works or we would not be doing it. But can we prove it? And do we need to? Our place in university hierarchies is often proof enough to us of what academic departments think of EAP! We work hard to improve and upgrade our students level of English so we must think it works, and we call it EAP in universities because we distinguish it from General English and tend to regard it as a part of ESP, But definitely proving it works is difficult if not impossible.

To conclude, could we possibly prove that it works? Well perhaps that brings me back to my failed attempt at research. Could we use empirical evidence to show that by taking a group of students with IELTS level 6.5 for example, and looking at one group of them who have had EAP courses, and another group who have not had any EAP courses and examine their degree success rate could we show if EAP works? How reliable would the results be because if the results of the two groups are the same that could show there is no real improvement, if the group who did not have EAP courses do badly and those who did EAP courses do well then we might claim that EAP probably affected their results, and if the group who had an EAP course did badly and the group who did not have an EAP course did well, then we probably would not want to share the results with anybody. In any case, for these results to be valid and reliable we would also need to take into account not only the variables previously mentioned, but other factors such as age, motivation, academic background, and perhaps a whole set of variables that might affect the results

So where do we go from here? Probably I have brought up more questions than answers. What I have tried to do is to make us think of ways in which we might answer the question "Does EAP work?" Perhaps we need to try to think of a reasonable research framework in which several institutions could participate. We could also discuss some of the issues raised through the BALEAP discussion forum. Three simple words "Does EAP work?" What a complex and almost unfathomable question we have asked. I can only leave it to you, fellow teachers, to see whether we can come up with any answers and where we go from here.

Notes on contributors

Barbara Atherton is a Senior Lecturer and the English Language Support Co-ordinator at Kingston University, where she is responsible for the design and delivery of the University's Pre and In-Sessional academic English language programmes. During her time at Kingston, Barbara has specialised in the design of discipline specific EAP materials and the role of feedback in the development of students' writing skills. In 2005, she was awarded a Kingston University Teaching Fellowship for a small scale research project assessing the effectiveness of Kingston's Pre-Sessional course.

Andy Gillett has spent most of the last 30 years teaching English both in the UK and abroad. During this time, he has taught mainly ESP - English for Specific Purposes - in universities, colleges, private language schools, offices and factories. For the last 20 years most of his work has been involved with English for Academic Purposes in British higher education. He is now mainly involved in organising, planning and teaching EAP courses to students taking a wide range of courses at the University of Hertfordshire. For several years, he has been involved with BALEAP and after spending two years as chair, he is now treasurer.

Simon Kinzley spent five-and-a-half years working in Japan as a TEFL teacher, a director of studies for a chain of private language schools and a part-time lecturer at the University of Tsukuba. He then returned to England where he did an MA in Language Teaching at Lancaster University. After graduating he went to China where he managed, taught on and went on to become the academic director for the entire country of the Northern Consortium of British Universities' international foundation year. The aim of this programme was to prepare young Chinese students for study at UK and Australian universities. He is currently doing a Ph.D. at Lancaster where he is looking at the relationship between adoption of academic writing practices taught on the university's Pre-Sessional course and levels of success achieved on undergraduate degree courses by students from the People's Republic of China. His main research interests are EAP and innovation theory.

Mary Martala is Senior Lecturer at the University of Hertfordshire with 18 years experience of teaching English both in UK and abroad. She was recently awarded an MA in Linguistics and English Language Teaching on which she researched the effectiveness of the EAP writing component taught to international students prior to entering their degree courses at the University of Hertfordshire. In her current post, she is responsible for the implementation of Integrated English to Modules across the University.

John Morley is responsible for running the University Language Centre's academic support programmes at Manchester. This role involves organising a wide variety of courses and workshops in English for Academic Purposes for international students and for home students. John has taught English in universities and schools in Australia, Singapore, Indonesia and Spain.

Nick Pilcher is a Teaching Fellow in the School of Management and Languages at Heriot-Watt University, Edinburgh. This paper is based on part of the results of his PhD studies which are currently ongoing at Heriot-Watt University

Diana Ridley has been involved in both teaching and research in the field of EAP at the University of Sheffield and Sheffield Hallam University since 1993. Prior to this, she taught EFL in Spain, worked at a teacher training college in Tanzania and provided language support in primary and secondary schools in the UK. Diana completed an MA in Linguistics for English Language Teaching in 1988 at Lancaster University. In 2004, she obtained her PhD at the University of Sheffield for which she researched the role of the PhD literature review. She has a continuing interest in research writing, genre analysis, the international student experience, and teaching and learning in higher education.

Sonya Saunders has been teaching and teacher-training for many years, mainly overseas. She has worked extensively at universities in Hong Kong, Israel, and Denmark and for the British Council on their ODA projects in China, Hungary and throughout the former Soviet Union. She did an MA in Applied Linguistics for English Language Teachers at Lancaster University. In August 2002 she joined the staff of the Language Centre at Royal Holloway, University of London. Her interests include content based EAP, materials writing for EAP, and intercultural communication.

Liz Wray is a Senior Lecturer at the University of Hertfordshire. She has experience of teaching English both overseas and in the UK. As well as teaching on a range of EAP programmes, she is responsible for the organisation and development of the Foundation Certificate in English for Academic Purposes programme. In September 2006 she completed an MA in Teaching English to Speakers of Other Languages at the Institute of Education.